CULTIVATING CHARACTER
An Islamic Lens to the Scout Law

by Younoos Latheef

MAS Publishing

Published by

MAS Publishing
712 H Street NE, Suite 1258
Washington, DC 20002
www.muslimamericansociety.org

1st Edition December 2022
ISBN 978-0-9792113-6-2

Printed in the U.S.A.
Designed by LRM Design

A Scout is ...

TRUSTWORTHY

LOYAL

HELPFUL

FRIENDLY

COURTEOUS

KIND

OBEDIENT

CHEERFUL

THRIFTY

BRAVE

CLEAN

REVERENT

To Mom and Dad who raised me
and provided me opportunities
to grow Islamically

Thank you to the individuals, scout troops, MAS chapters, and youth leaders who sponsored this book.

May Allah reward them immensely!

Muslim American Society (MAS)
Houston Chapter

MAS Scouting Unit 713 (Houston, TX)

Omar Albustami

Mohammad Awad

Reshad Noorzay

Abbas Selmane

Several Anonymous Kind Souls

Preface

"The most beloved people to Allah are those with the best character."

    – Prophet Muhammad (s)

From an early age, my beloved parents and my dear mentors impressed upon me the importance of good character as exhibited by the Prophet Muhammad (s). As I grew older and served as a mentor myself, I continued stressing good character as an essential component to one's Islamic development. I had an opportunity to further my interest and passion in Islamic character building when the MAS Scouting Unit 713 was formed, and I was asked to serve as its first chaplain. As a scout leader, I was always seeking ways to develop the scouts' Islamic personality, whether it be teaching a *dua* for building confidence or sharing the Islamic perspective on a current event.

After serving the unit in various capacities over eight years, I noticed an opportunity to assist chaplains and scout leaders in preparing Islamic content to share with their scouts. As a leader and mentor, you typically do not have the time to prepare Islamic messages to incorporate in your program. This book provides an Islamic lens to twelve universal characteristics (i.e. the Scout Law) which can be easily adapted for Girl Scouts, youth groups, Islamic studies teachers and even adults.

The book is intended to cultivate a Muslim youth's character by connecting them with Allah and the Quran, sayings of the Prophet (s) and inspirational stories from Islam's role models. Additionally, we have incorporated thought-provoking reflection questions and activities to further develop the young Muslim's understanding. Finally, we introduced supplications that Muslim youth can use to seek Allah's guidance in embodying good character.

This book would not be possible without, first, the help of Allah and then the many scout leaders who supported me along the way. I would especially like to thank Amr Ahmed (Scoutmaster Troop 713), Siddiq Qidwai (Committee Chair Troop 1576) and Nadim Islam (Charter Organization Representative Unit 713) for their continued support and encouragement. In addition, I want to thank Maha Ezzeddine as the chief editor and Louise Magruder as the graphic designer. Finally, I want to thank my wife, Fathima, and my children (Z³) for their unyielding support. I hope Allah accepts this effort as a *sadaqa jariya* (continuous charity) for all those who assisted in any way.

Purpose

The aim of this book is to help youth leaders develop their youths' Islamic personality while instilling the principles of the BSA Scout Law. Each chapter explores a character trait from the Islamic perspective and is divided into the following sections on the right.

A Scout is...

Contents

1. What do Allah and His Prophet (s) say about being ...?

Used for Leader or youth talk

2. What does it mean again?

3. Tell me a story

Inspiring stories to be told around campfires

4. What's in it for me?

Used for Leader or youth talk

5. Let's do this

Activities to build character

6. Let's reflect

Thought-provoking questions for meetings or campfires

7. Let's make dua

Dua to be memorized or read after meetings or during campfires

8. Let's teach it

Suggested curriculum for easy planning

How to use this book

A Scout is....

The opening paragraph is the character trait's definition from the Scout Handbook. This is followed by a brief summary of additional aspects from the Islamic perspective. This section concludes with some names or attributes of Allah that are connected with the character trait so that youth can emulate.

What do Allah and His Prophet (s) say about being...?

This section highlights what Allah says in the Quran about a certain character trait. Some or all of these verses can be read along with their translation at the start of a meeting. They can also be the subject of a short talk presented by an adult leader or youth. In addition, each section lists authentic hadiths on what the Prophet Muhammad (s) said or how he modeled the behavior trait. These sayings can also be used as topics for short talks.

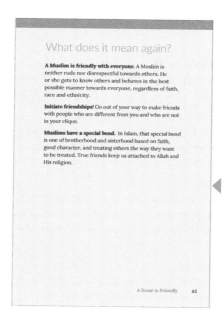

What does it mean again?

A Muslim is friendly with everyone. A Muslim is neither rude nor disrespectful towards others. He or she gets to know others and behaves in the best possible manner towards everyone, regardless of faith, race and ethnicity.

Initiate friendships! Go out of your way to make friends with people who are different from you and who are not in your clique.

Muslims have a special bond. In Islam, that special bond is one of brotherhood and sisterhood based on faith, good character, and treating others the way they want to be treated. True friends keep us attached to Allah and His religion.

A Scout is Friendly   61

What does it mean again?

Summarizes the Islamic perspective in a few brief points which can be used to introduce the character in a short talk.

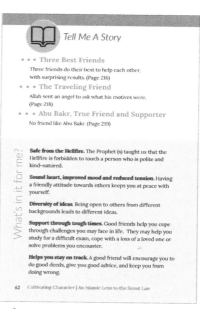

Tell Me A Story

• • • **Three Best Friends**
Three friends do their best to help each other, with surprising results. (Page 216)

• • • **The Traveling Friend**
Allah sent an angel to ask what his motives were. (Page 218)

• • • **Abu Bakr, True Friend and Supporter**
No friend like Abu Bakr. (Page 219)

What's in it for me?

Safe from the Hellfire. The Prophet (s) taught us that the Hellfire is forbidden to touch a person who is polite and kind-natured.

Sound heart, improved mood and reduced tension. Having a friendly attitude towards others keeps you at peace with yourself.

Diversity of ideas. Being open to others from different backgrounds leads to different ideas.

Support through tough times. Good friends help you cope through challenges you may face in life. They may help you study for a difficult exam, cope with a loss of a loved one or solve problems you encounter.

Helps you stay on track. A good friend will encourage you to do good deeds, give you good advice, and keep you from doing wrong.

62   Cultivating Character | An Islamic Lens to the Scout Law

Tell me a story

Inspirational stories found in the Islamic tradition that can be shared around a campfire or during a short talk. Stories give life and meaning to the traits and should be retold with enthusiasm. Many of the stories can be used to exemplify multiple character traits, as represented by the icons next to each story title. We have compiled the stories at the end of the book to moderate the length of each chapter.

What's in it for me?

All behavior change is a result of motivation. This section expresses the motivation for a youth to exhibit the behavior. Youth need to hear that adhering to these character traits will not only benefit him or her in the Hereafter, but also in this life.

Let's do this

• • • Not So Friendly Feelings

This is an activity to help youth empathize with those who may not have as many friends. Distribute index cards to the group. As you read out each scenario below, each group should write down expressions describing how a person might feel in each situation and add them to the container. After each question, read the responses and discuss. Example of scenarios:

1. Being the last to be chosen for a team.

2. Not finding a partner for a classroom activity.

3. You see your friend but he is busy, doesn't smile, and doesn't seem to notice you.

4. Telling a joke or doing a stunt and no one laughs or seems interested.

5. Sitting in the mosque gym where a lot of kids are playing but no one invites you to join their game.

6. Saying salam but no one responds.

(Supplies: Index cards, container to hold the index cards)

• • • Speed Chatting

Make a list of a few prompts and opening lines you can use to strike up a conversation with a stranger or new friend. The goal is to develop skill in striking conversation with someone they don't know. Set a timer for 90 seconds, have youth

A Scout is Friendly   63

Let's do this

Youth learn best by doing. Hence, this section presents activities that foster the moral values intended by the Scout Law. Most activities can be conducted during a scout or youth meeting or campout. Others are for youth to do on their own. Regardless, to maximize effectiveness, the activities should be followed by a debrief with the youth to reflect on their learnings. We have included sufficient activities to provide variety that can span several seasons.

Let's reflect

1. Reflect on your friends and those you hang out with. Do you have a diverse group of friends from different ethnicities and socio-economic backgrounds? Why or why not?

2. What are some positive characteristics of good friends? Bad friends?

3. Is it better to be alone or to mix with the people? Explain.

4. In your opinion, what tears apart friendships? Explain.

5. Name some practical actions you can do to be friendly to all.

6. What is the difference between acquaintances, friends, and true friends?

7. When might you feel uncomfortable befriending someone? Explain.

8. What names and attributes of Allah remind us of the importance of being friendly to others? Discuss how Allah is Al-Lateef (The Gentle and Friendly), Al-Waali (The Protector), Al-Waliy (The Guardian), An-Naseer (The Helpful) and how we can channel those names of Allah in our daily lives.

66   Cultivating Character | An Islamic Lens to the Scout Law

Let's reflect

To deeply appreciate a character trait, youth need opportunities to think and discuss the trait with their fellow youth and leaders. In this section, you will find stimulating questions which can be asked around a campfire, during a hike or in a meeting to challenge the youth's understanding. Additionally, the last question of this section asks the youth to reflect on the character with respect to Allah's names and attributes.

Let's make dua.
Imagine a youth reciting daily supplications to be granted these character traits. The intent of this section is to connect youth to Allah through *dua* (supplications). My recommendation is to focus on learning one supplication a month which should be recited aloud at the end of each meeting or after each prayer. Encourage your youth to recite the *dua* on their own after each prayer so it becomes a habit.

Let's teach it
The content for each trait can easily span 2-3 months, but I suggest focusing on a trait for each month. In each section, I have included a suggested curriculum for each character to simplify your preparation. The curriculum outlines week by week how each section can be incorporated into your meetings and campouts.

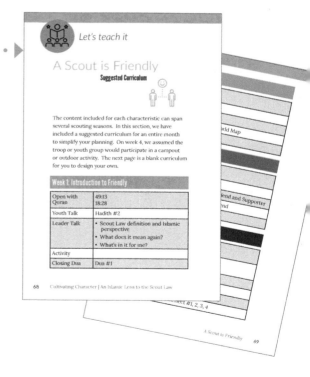

● ● ● A Youth-Led Approach for Scouting

I realize that each troop has varying degrees of what it means to be boy- or girl-led. However, we all know that scouting is most effective when it is youth-led. I encourage troops to have their scout chaplains and senior patrol leader lead the implementation of this curriculum with the supervision of the adult chaplain and scout master.

Supplemental Content
Scan for supplemental resources to assist in using the material.

● ● ● We would love to hear from you!

If you would like to schedule a training session with the author on how best to use this book, would like to share your feedback, or if you found any errors with the text, feel free to contact us at *character@muslimamericansociety.org.*

Glossary

Allah: the Arabic name for God

Ayah: a verse of the Quran

Companions: Those who converted to Islam and lived alongside Prophet Muhammad (s)

Dua: a supplication or prayer that calls upon Allah and asks of Him

Fitrah: the good, pure, and natural state upon which human beings were created

Hadith: a saying of Prophet Muhammad (s) transmitted through a chain of narrators. The sayings and traditions of the Prophet (s) were meticulously recorded and verified after his death

Quran: the final revelation from God to all of mankind, sent through Prophet Muhammad (s)

Salah: prayer; the fifth pillar of Islam

(s): this signifies, "May God's peace and blessings be upon him," (*Salla Allah wa alaihi wa sallam*) which is a prayer said whenever Prophet Muhammad (s) is mentioned

Sunnah: the example set by Prophet Muhammad (s) which all Muslims should strive to follow as best as they can

Surah: a chapter of the Quran

Wudu: a ritual washing before prayer

A Scout is Trustworthy

A Scout is trustworthy. A Scout tells the truth. A Scout is honest and keeps promises. People can depend on a Scout. Trustworthiness will help you make and maintain good friendships. As you demonstrate that you are trustworthy, you are showing your character—the person you are on the inside. If your judgment fails and you make a mistake, your good character will be what helps you quickly admit it and make good on any damage. Adults and your peers alike will know that they can rely on you to do your best in every situation. Living in this way also means that you can trust yourself. (The Scout Handbook)

Trustworthiness is such an essential characteristic of a Muslim and was a quality of all the prophets. Our beloved Prophet Muhammad (s) was known to the people as As-Sadiq (the Truthful) and Al-Amin (the Trustworthy). In Islam, honesty begins with Allah. When we say the testimony of faith, we honestly believe in it from our heart, and we trust that Allah will save us from entering the Hellfire.

Allah is Al-Wakeel, The Trustee, and Al-Haqq, The Absolute Truth. We entrust Him with our affairs, doing our part and leaving the result to Al-Wakeel. Allah is the ultimate truth; He is true and everything about Him is true including His Books, His Messengers, His Rewards and His Punishment.

What do Allah and the Prophet (s) say about being trustworthy?

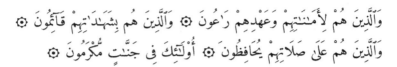

• • • • • In the Quran

وَالَّذِينَ هُمْ لِأَمَٰنَٰتِهِمْ وَعَهْدِهِمْ رَٰعُونَ ۞ وَالَّذِينَ هُم بِشَهَٰدَٰتِهِمْ قَآئِمُونَ ۞ وَالَّذِينَ هُمْ عَلَىٰ صَلَاتِهِمْ يُحَافِظُونَ ۞ أُوْلَٰٓئِكَ فِى جَنَّٰتٍ مُّكْرَمُونَ ۞

Those who keep their trusts and honor their promises, who stand firm in their testimonies, and who strictly guard their prayers. It is they who shall live with honor in Paradise. (70:32-35)

يَٰٓأَيُّهَا الَّذِينَ ءَامَنُواْ اتَّقُواْ اللَّهَ وَكُونُواْ مَعَ الصَّٰدِقِينَ ۞

You who believe! Be mindful of Allah and be with those who are truthful! (9:119)

يَٰٓأَيُّهَا الَّذِينَ ءَامَنُواْ لِمَ تَقُولُونَ مَا لَا تَفْعَلُونَ كَبُرَ مَقْتًا عِندَ اللَّهِ أَن تَقُولُواْ مَا لَا تَفْعَلُونَ ۞

You who believe, why do you say things and then do not do them? It is most hateful to Allah that you say things and then do not do them. (61:2-3)

يَٰٓأَيُّهَا الَّذِينَ ءَامَنُواْ لَا تَأْكُلُوٓاْ أَمْوَٰلَكُم بَيْنَكُم بِالْبَٰطِلِ

You who believe, do not wrongfully consume each other's wealth ... (4:29)

وَيْلٌ لِّلْمُطَفِّفِينَ ۝ الَّذِينَ إِذَا اكْتَالُواْ عَلَى النَّاسِ يَسْتَوْفُونَ ۝ وَإِذَا كَالُوهُمْ أُو
وَّزَنُوهُمْ يُخْسِرُونَ ۝ أَلَا يَظُنُّ أُولَئِكَ أَنَّهُم مَّبْعُوثُونَ ۝ لِيَوْمٍ عَظِيمٍ ۝ يَوْمَ يَقُومُ
النَّاسُ لِرَبِّ الْعَالَمِينَ ۝

Woe to those who give short measure, who demand of
other people full measure for themselves, but when it
is they who weigh or measure for others give less than
they should. Do these people not realize that they will
be raised up on a mighty Day, a Day when everyone will
stand before the Lord of the Worlds. (83: 1-6)

In the Hadith

1. "Honesty certainly leads to goodness, and goodness
   leads to Paradise. Truly, a man keeps speaking the
   truth until he is inscribed as being true through
   and through. And lying leads to wickedness, and
   wickedness leads to Hell. Truly, a man lies and lies
   until he is inscribed as being a liar through and
   through." (Muslim)

2. "The signs of a hypocrite are three: when he speaks,
   he lies, when he promises, he breaks it, and when he
   is trusted, he betrays." (Bukhari)

3. "Assure six deeds for me, and I will assure you
   Paradise. When you speak, do not lie. When you
   promise, do not break it. When you are trusted, do
   not betray. Lower your gaze, guard your chastity,
   and restrain your hands from harming others."
   (Tabarani)

4. "There is no faith for one who cannot be trusted. There is no religion for one who cannot uphold a covenant." (Ahmad)

5. The Prophet of Allah (s) once came upon a heap of corn in the market of Medina and thrust his hands into it. His fingers felt damp. Upon being asked, the trader replied that rain had fallen upon it. The Prophet (s) said, "Why did you not then keep (the wet portion of) it above the dry corn, so that people may see it? He who deceives is not one of us." (Muslim)

What does it mean again?

Our word is golden. A scout keeps his or her promises even during difficult circumstances. This is one of the greatest and defining characteristics of the Muslim.

Always follow through. When we assume a responsibility, we can be counted on to deliver.

Honesty is our way of life. Honesty is in everything we do, from being sincere in our worship of Allah to being truthful with ourselves and others by speaking and interacting honestly.

Taking care of others' possessions. When borrowing or being entrusted with someone's belongings, we return things in the proper condition in which we received them.

Tell Me A Story

What's in it for me?

A house in Paradise. The Prophet (s) said, "I guarantee a house on the outskirts of Paradise, a house in the middle of Paradise, and a house in the highest part of Paradise for one who gives up arguing even when he is right, who gives up lying even while joking, and who makes his character excellent." (Tabarani)

Strengthens your leadership. People follow leaders they can trust, and leaders can influence people more when they are trusted.

Others like to deal with you. People like to deal with those they can trust. You like to shop at a store where you know that the owner or salesperson will deal with you honestly. Supervisors like to hire workers they know will be reliable. If people trust you, they will like you and give you more responsibility.

Confidence. Honest people trust themselves. Never underestimate the life-changing power of the ability to trust yourself. When you are honest, do as promised, and can handle responsibility, you feel self-respect, knowing that you are worthy of others' trust.

Less stress, peaceful heart and mind. Pretending to be something you are not requires constant attention to detail. Speaking the truth prevents you from feelings of anxiety over being 'found out' and worrying about covering your tracks. Honest people are better able to relax. They are just being themselves and so naturally feel better.

Closer friendships. Honesty and integrity pave the way for greater intimacy. Your friends love the true "you," not the fake "you."

Let's do this

• • • Willow in the Wind

This activity emphasizes trust within a team. Select a person to be the "willow" standing in a center of a circle with their feet together in a rigid, upright position. The rest of the team forms a tight circle around the willow with each member standing with one foot in front of the other, arms outstretched, elbows locked ready to pass the willow around. The willow trusting their team closes his or her eyes and leans in any direction allowing the spotters to pass them around the circle. Each team member is encouraged to have a turn in the middle. (*Caution: Adults should supervise closely to safeguard the youth falling in the middle*) Some discussion questions:

1. How does it feel being the willow trusting your team?

2. How does it feel being on the outside responsible for the willow?

3. Describe any fears you had during the activity.

4. The willow relied on the team. How can we support each other while working on a task or in life?

5. What can we do to help others feel comfortable trusting us?

6. What would happen if you did not trust your team? Why is trust important?

Source: Creative Youth Ideas

Read more at *https://masnational.org/p7d*

● ● ● Snakes

Snakes is a teambuilding activity that helps youth practice trusting each other. The objective of the game is to place an item into the bucket. Create a large circle barrier with tape or a rope, with throwable items scattered inside and a bucket in the middle. Organize youth into teams of 5-7 people who are all blindfolded except for the leader who can see and is positioned at the end of the line. All players hold on to each other's shoulders in the form of a snake. The seeing leader, positioned at the end of the line, leads the snake around the circle barrier by tapping the shoulders of the person in front of them, who will tap the shoulders of the person in front of them. The objective is to guide the snake to pick up an object in the circle and then drop it into a bucket. This is a no-talking activity, but teams are allowed 1-2 minutes to pre-plan and agree on different signals (stop, right, left, etc). Once an item is successfully deposited in the bucket, team players can switch roles so that everyone gets a chance to be the seeing leader. Alternatively, it can be organized as a competition between teams. Debrief by asking: How the team established trust with each other? What strategies did the team use? Why or why wasn't the team successful? (*Supplies: blindfolds, throwable items, buckets, rope or tape, stopwatch*) **Source: LRNG**

Read more at https://masnational.org/snakes

• • • Check yourself!

This exercise helps youth reflect on their level of honesty. Ask each youth to privately rate how honest they are: 1=I often lie, 2=Sometimes, I lie, and 3=I always tell the truth.

Encourage youth, if comfortable, to share their responses to the following:

1. Give an example of when it was hard to tell the truth.

2. Why did you choose to be truthful, although lying would have been easier?

3 What's one area where you could be more honest? Think about honesty with your parents, siblings, friends, at school, etc. Share an example where you may not tell all the details to hide the truth.

4. How does telling a lie make you feel on the inside?

Source: Drake University

Read more at https://masnational.org/lies

• • • Piggyback Rider Obstacle

This activity tests one's communication skills and the level of trust between partners. Divide the group into threes where one person will be the obstacle thrower; one will be the piggyback rider; and the third person is the walker or carrier who is blindfolded. Using a rope as a boundary, designate a path where the obstacle thrower will toss obstacles and the rider and carrier must walk through. As the walker carries the rider, the obstacle thrower tosses obstacles 5 to 10 feet in front of the walker with enough time for the walker-rider pair to react. Using verbal commands, the rider guides the blindfolded walker to avoid obstacles and make it to the end. Switch roles allowing everyone to experience being the walker. Debrief with the group on the importance of trust between the rider and the walker. (*Supplies: Blindfold, obstacles, rope, large area*) **Source: Love to Know**

Read more at https://masnational.org/teens

● ● ● Cake Demonstration

In this activity, youth learn that dishonesty cannot be hidden and forgotten. Make sure everyone has permission to eat cake and consider any food allergies in the group. Distribute a small bowl of plain cake to everyone and have them enjoy a bite. Ask them how it tasted and explain that telling a lie can ruin a good thing. Next, have each person pour some salt on their cake and try it again. Lastly, let everyone drizzle chocolate syrup over the salt and taste the cake once more. Compare the salt to telling a lie. You can try to cover it by doing something good, but it's difficult to repair the trust that you lost. Discuss how one might build back trust that was lost. Be sure to bring some extra cake for everyone to enjoy to get rid of the salty taste. (*Supplies: plain cake, salt, chocolate syrup, bowls*) **Source: Positivepsychology.com**

Read more at https://masnational.org/hya

Let's reflect

1. When you realize that someone has lied to you, how does that affect your relationship with that person?

2. Why is it so tempting to lie? What characteristics come to mind when thinking of a dishonest person?

3. If someone lies to you and asks forgiveness, do you let it go? What if they do it again?

4. What are ways people lie on social media? How does that affect others? Themselves?

5. How does lying impact my future?

6. How do you earn someone's trust?

7. How hard is it to build back your trust with someone?

8. Share an example of when you broke someone's trust. How did it make you feel? Were you able to earn it back? If yes, how?

9. How is Allah truthful to us? What does it mean to entrust our affairs to Allah? What names and attributes of Allah remind us of the importance of being trustworthy? Discuss how Allah is *Al-Haqq* (The Truth) and *Al-Wakeel* (The Trustworthy) and how we can channel those names of Allah in our daily lives.

Let's make dua

1. "Allah is sufficient for me. There is no God but He. I have placed my trust in Him, He is Lord of the Majestic Throne." Whoever says this seven times in the morning after Fajr, and seven times after Asr, Allah will take care of whatever worries him of the matter of this world and the Hereafter. (Muslim)

حَسْبِيَ اللهُ لآ إِلَهَ إِلّا هُوَ عَلَيْهِ تَوَكَّلْتُ وَهُوَ رَبُّ الْعَرْشِ الْعَظِيمِ

2. The Prophet (s) said: "Whoever says when he leaves his house, 'In the name of Allah, I put my trust in Allah and there is no power and no strength except with Allah,' it will be said to him: 'You are taken care of and you are protected and guided,' and the devils will move away from him, and one devil will say: 'What can you do to a man who has been guided, taken care of and protected?" (Abu Dawood)

بِسْم اللهِ تَوَكَّلْتُ عَلَى اللهِ وَلا حوْلَ وَلا قُوةَ إلاَّ بِاللهِ

3. O Allah, I ask you for steadfastness in this matter, and I ask You for the resolve to adhere to the path of guidance, and I ask You for gratitude for Your blessings and to worship You well, and I ask You for a truthful tongue and a sound heart. (an-Nasa'i)

اللّهُمَّ إِنِّي أَسْأَلُكَ الثَّبَاتَ فِي الْأَمْرِ وَأَسْأَلُكَ عَزِيمَةَ الرُّشْدِ وَأَسْأَلُكَ شُكْرَ نِعْمَتِكَ وَحُسْنَ عِبَادَتِكَ وَأَسْأَلُكَ لِسَانًا صَادِقًا وَقَلْبًا سَلِيمًا

Let's teach it

A Scout is Trustworthy

Suggested Curriculum

The content included for each characteristic can span several scouting seasons. In this section, we have included a suggested curriculum for an entire month to simplify your planning. On week 4, we assumed the troop or youth group would participate in a campout or outdoor activity. The next section is a blank curriculum for you to design your own.

Week 1: Introduction to Trustworthy

Open with Quran	70:32-35
Youth Talk	Hadith #3
Leader Talk	• Scout Law definition and Islamic perspective • What does it mean again? • What's in it for me?
Activity	Check Yourself
Closing Dua	Dua #1

Week 2: Honesty

Open with Quran	9:119
Youth Talk	Hadith #1
Leader Talk	A Shining Reputation
Activity	Let's Reflect #1, 2, 3
Closing Dua	Dua #1

Week 3: Dependable

Open with Quran	61:2-3
Youth Talk	Hadith #4
Leader Talk	A Trustworthy Tax Return
Activity	Let's Reflect #6, 7, 8
Closing Dua	Dua #1

Week 4 Camp: Bringing it All Together

Open with Quran	70:32-35
Youth Talk	• Hadith #5 • Let's Reflect #9
Leader Talk	The Repentant Robber
Activity	Willow in the Wind
Closing Dua	Dua #1 (After each prayer)
Campfire	Let's Reflect #4, 5

Let's teach it

A Scout is Trustworthy

Design your own Curriculum

Week 1:

Open with Quran	
Youth Talk	
Leader Talk	
Activity	
Closing Dua	

Week 2:

Open with Quran	
Youth Talk	
Leader Talk	
Activity	
Closing Dua	

Week 3:

Open with Quran	
Youth Talk	
Leader Talk	
Activity	
Closing Dua	

Week 4 Camp:

Open with Quran	
Youth Talk	
Leader Talk	
Activity	
Closing Dua	
Campfire	

A Scout is Loyal

A Scout is loyal. A Scout is loyal to those to whom loyalty is due. A Scout shows that he or she cares about their family, friends, scout leaders, school, and country. Loyalty can be shown everywhere: at home, in your troop and patrol, among your classmates at school. You can also express loyalty to the United States when you respect the flag and the government. Give real meaning to your loyalty by helping to improve your community, state and nation. (The Scout Handbook)

In Islam, loyalty is first due to Allah and His Messenger by adhering to the teachings and values of the faith. Allah commands us to be righteous and just, which guides our loyalty to others. We practice loyalty to people including our family, friends and community by supporting, caring, maintaining relationships, and defending them. In Islam, loyalty to people, even those most dear to us, has a limit when it conflicts with what is true and just.

Allah is *Al-Wali*, The Protector. He guards and protects us in the most loving manner. We can rely on Him to be there for us, to answer when we call upon Him, and to help us through our problems. Being loyal to truth and justice and those on earth can be difficult, so the Muslim relies on Allah's guardianship to get him or her through those struggles. Allah is *As-Samad*, The Eternal, Self-Sufficient. He is constantly supporting and sustaining us and deserves our complete loyalty. Some of the ways that we can express loyalty to Allah is by following His religion, remembering His blessings in the past and present, and being grateful and thanking Him every day.

What do Allah and the Prophet (s) say about being loyal?

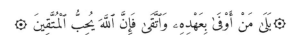

In the Quran

۞ بَلَىٰ مَنْ أَوْفَىٰ بِعَهْدِهِۦ وَٱتَّقَىٰ فَإِنَّ ٱللَّهَ يُحِبُّ ٱلْمُتَّقِينَ ۞

Yes, whoever fulfills his covenant and is mindful —then
indeed, Allah loves mindful people. (3:76)

وَبِعَهْدِ ٱللَّهِ أَوْفُوا۟ ذَٰلِكُمْ وَصَّىٰكُم بِهِۦ لَعَلَّكُمْ تَذَكَّرُونَ ۞

... And fulfill your covenant with Allah. This is what He has
commanded you, so perhaps you will remember. (6:152)

ٱللَّهُ وَلِىُّ ٱلَّذِينَ ءَامَنُوا۟ يُخْرِجُهُم مِّنَ ٱلظُّلُمَٰتِ إِلَى ٱلنُّورِ

Allah is the protector of those who believe, He takes
them out of darkness into light... (2:257)

أَلَآ إِنَّ أَوْلِيَآءَ ٱللَّهِ لَا خَوْفٌ عَلَيْهِمْ وَلَا هُمْ يَحْزَنُونَ ۞ ٱلَّذِينَ ءَامَنُوا۟ وَكَانُوا۟
يَتَّقُونَ ۞ لَهُمُ ٱلْبُشْرَىٰ فِى ٱلْحَيَوٰةِ ٱلدُّنْيَا وَفِى ٱلْءَاخِرَةِ

But for those who are on Allah's side there is no fear,
nor shall they grieve. For those who believe and are
conscious of Allah, for them there is good news in this life
and in the Hereafter... (10:62-64)

قُلْ إِن كُنتُمْ تُحِبُّونَ ٱللَّهَ فَٱتَّبِعُونِي يُحْبِبْكُمُ ٱللَّهُ وَيَغْفِرْ لَكُمْ ذُنُوبَكُمْ ۗ وَٱللَّهُ غَفُورٌ رَّحِيمٌ ۞

Say, (O Prophet) "If you sincerely love Allah, then follow me; Allah will love you and forgive your sins. For Allah is All-Forgiving, Most Merciful." (3:31)

يَـٰٓأَيُّهَا ٱلَّذِينَ ءَامَنُوا۟ كُونُوا۟ قَوَّٰمِينَ بِٱلْقِسْطِ شُهَدَآءَ لِلَّهِ وَلَوْ عَلَىٰٓ أَنفُسِكُمْ أَوِ ٱلْوَٰلِدَيْنِ وَٱلْأَقْرَبِينَ ۚ إِن يَكُنْ غَنِيًّا أَوْ فَقِيرًا فَٱللَّهُ أَوْلَىٰ بِهِمَا ۖ فَلَا تَتَّبِعُوا۟ ٱلْهَوَىٰٓ أَن تَعْدِلُوا۟ ۚ وَإِن تَلْوُۥٓا۟ أَوْ تُعْرِضُوا۟ فَإِنَّ ٱللَّهَ كَانَ بِمَا تَعْمَلُونَ خَبِيرًا ۞

O believers! Stand firm for justice as witnesses for Allah even if it is against yourselves, your parents, or close relatives. Be they rich or poor, Allah is best to ensure their interests. So do not let your desires cause you to deviate [from justice]. If you distort the testimony or refuse to give it, then [know that] Allah is certainly All-Aware of what you do. (4:135)

وَٱخْفِضْ لَهُمَا جَنَاحَ ٱلذُّلِّ مِنَ ٱلرَّحْمَةِ وَقُل رَّبِّ ٱرْحَمْهُمَا كَمَا رَبَّيَانِي صَغِيرًا ۞

And be humble with them out of mercy, and pray, "My Lord! Be merciful to them as they raised me when I was young." (17:24)

إِنَّمَا ٱلْمُؤْمِنُونَ إِخْوَةٌ فَأَصْلِحُوا۟ بَيْنَ أَخَوَيْكُمْ ۚ وَٱتَّقُوا۟ ٱللَّهَ لَعَلَّكُمْ تُرْحَمُونَ ۞

The believers are but one brotherhood, so make peace between your brothers. And be mindful of Allah so you may be shown mercy. (49:10)

لَّا يَنْهَىٰكُمُ ٱللَّهُ عَنِ ٱلَّذِينَ لَمْ يُقَـٰتِلُوكُمْ فِى ٱلدِّينِ وَلَمْ يُخْرِجُوكُم مِّن دِيَـٰرِكُمْ أَن تَبَرُّوهُمْ وَتُقْسِطُوٓا۟ إِلَيْهِمْ ۚ إِنَّ ٱللَّهَ يُحِبُّ ٱلْمُقْسِطِينَ ۝

Allah does not forbid you from dealing kindly and fairly with those who have neither fought nor driven you out of your homes. Surely, Allah loves those who are fair. (60:8)

• • • • • In the Hadith

1. "I enjoin you to have God-consciousness and that you listen and obey, even if a slave is made a ruler over you. He among you who lives long enough will see many differences. So observe my Sunnah and the Sunnah of the rightly-principled and rightly-guided successors, holding on to them with your molar teeth..." (Abu Dawud)

2. One day Aisha, mother of the believers, saw the Prophet (s) praying the night prayer until his feet swelled. She asked him why he did so, when Allah had forgiven all of his sins? He said to her, "Should not I be a thankful servant?" (Bukhari)

3. The Prophet (s) said, "I wish I could meet my brothers." His Companions asked, "Are we not your brothers?" The Prophet (s) said, "You are my Companions, but my brothers are those who have faith in me although they never saw me." (Ahmad)

4. "Help your brother, whether he is an oppressor or oppressed." People asked, "O Allah's Messenger!

It is all right to help him if he is oppressed, but how should we help him if he is an oppressor?" The Prophet (s) said, "By stopping him from oppressing others." (Bukhari)

5. "The bond of relationship is suspended from the Throne, declaring: "He who keeps good relations with me, Allah will keep a connection with him, but whoever severs relations with me, Allah will sever connection with him." (Bukhari)

6. "Don't cut ties of kinship. Don't bear enmity against one another, don't avoid one another, and don't feel envy toward each other. Live as fellow brothers, as Allah commands you." (Muslim)

7. "The one who keeps good relations with family is not the one who is reciprocated. Rather, the one who keeps good relations with family is one who does so despite being cut off by them." (Bukhari)

8. "A believer is like a brick for another believer, each one supporting the other." (Bukhari)

9. "A Muslim is the brother of a Muslim; he does not oppress him, nor fail him, nor lie to him, nor does he hold his brother in contempt." (Muslim)

10. Asma' bint Abu Bakr said, "My mother visited me while she was still worshiping idols, so I asked the Prophet (s), 'My mother has come to visit me and she is hoping for my favor. Shall I maintain good relations with her?' He (s) replied, 'Yes! Maintain good relations with your mother." (Bukhari)

What does it mean again?

Showing loyalty to Allah and the Prophet. Because we are loyal to Allah above all else, we love what Allah loves and avoid what Allah hates. We express loyalty to the Prophet (s) by following his Sunnah.

A Muslim is loyal to justice. A Muslim is loyal to what is true and just, no matter how unpopular or uncomfortable that might be.

A Muslim is always there for family. Family is one of our greatest blessings on earth. A Muslim appreciates all the good family does and doesn't forget to serve and thank his or her parents. We also look out for our siblings and support them when they need us.

A Muslim supports their friends and troop. A Muslim doesn't forget when someone befriends him or her or does something nice. Mulims make sure to not abandon their friends or let them down. Just because someone makes a mistake or causes us some harm, we should not ignore all of the good they have done previously.

Supports leadership by advising and not undermining. A Muslim supports and promotes the plans of the troop or youth group, even when they are not his or her favorite choice. If something should be changed, the Muslim seeks the proper channels to advise and propose an alternative solution.

Tell Me A Story

• • • **High and Low Company**

The nobles of Quraish look down on the early Muslims. (pg. 209)

• • • **Loyalty to Khadijah**

The Prophet (s) never forgot his wife, even after she passed away. (pg. 210)

• • • **Youth of the Cave**

Together they gave up everything to protect their faith. (pg. 211)

What's in it for me?

Protection and comfort in the next life. When we obey Allah and remember Him often in this life, He will take care of us and remember us in the next life.

Happier & healthier. Having loyalty to friends and the troop or youth group makes you laugh and relax, easing tension and leading to a healthier mind and body.

Support during tough times. A loyal friend or family member will be there when you need help or advice in tackling a sticky situation.

More fun. There is not much fun in being alone. Friends and family who stick by your side make life fun and enjoyable.

Let's do this

• • • Learning to Lean

Divide youth into an even number, ideally 6 or 8 per group. Each group stands in a circle holding hands, or wrists to make the circle stronger, and counts off in order: one, two, one, two. Instruct the youth: "When I say 'Go!' all the "ones" lean forward while the "twos" lean back. Hold tightly to support each other from falling." Next, ask them to reverse: the youth leaning forward to lean backward and so on. Some discussion questions:

1. Was it hard for you to trust the others when you leaned forward and back? Why? How many of you were a little scared?

2. Why is it important to be able to trust the people who are holding you?

3. If a person is loyal, how will that change how they hold on to you?

4. Did you like depending on each other? Supporting each other?

5. What would have happened if someone dropped their hands?

6. In real life, how do we lean on each other for support? How do we show our loyalty to each other?

Source: Greater Good in Education

• • • Loyalty to Country

Invite a veteran, first responder, or community official to speak on what loyalty means to them during and outside of their service. In addition, discuss how loyalty is expressed in a family, among friends, or on a team. What are some examples of where loyalty can be harmful? **Source: Character Council**

Read more at *https://masnational.org/wvh*

• • • Gladiator Balloon Battle

This game will test one's loyalty to their partner. Divide the group into pairs and allocate an indoor room with clear boundaries where youth can run. Ask each pair to tie the middle of their legs together. Then, give each person 6 balloons to blow up and link them together on a string which they will tie to their other ankle. There should be a few inches between each balloon on the string. The objective of the game is to pop everyone's balloons by stomping on them while keeping your own balloons from getting stomped. The person (not pair!) who has the most balloons still blown up on their ankle, wins. However, do remember that your partner will also try to have balloons still blown up by the end of the game. All balloons must be on the ground and cannot be held up or hidden. When you and your partner's balloons are all popped, you are out. The game begins when I say, "Go."

During the debrief, ask:

1. What strategies did you employ during this game? Which ones were successful?

2. Were you tempted to betray your partner? Explain.

3. Was loyalty a factor in this game? Explain.

Source: Ministry to Youth

Read more at *https://masnational.org/loyalty*

Let's reflect

1. What does it look like to be loyal to Allah and to His Prophet (s)?

2. How can we be more loyal to our troop or youth group members?

3. What does it mean to be disloyal to your family, troop, friends, or Allah? We may think that we would never be disloyal, but what are some of the subtle, everyday ways we might be disloyal? Examples: Not sticking up for a friend that is being mistreated or bullied, not defending a family member if they are being put down, not obeying certain laws.

4. We often take our siblings for granted. What are some ways we can be more loyal to them?

5. What are some of the negative support systems that some people get into? What are some of the positive support systems that we belong to?

6. Rate these questions from 1 to 10: how important is loyalty in a friend? How loyal would you say that you are? How tough is it to find a friend who is truly loyal these days?

7. Think about all of the friends that you have—who do you trust without question? Don't say it out loud, but do share how you know that you can trust them.

8. "Loyalty is the brother of truth and justice." What do you think of this saying and what might it mean?

9. What names and attributes of Allah remind us of
   the importance of loyalty? Discuss how Allah is
   Al-Wali (The Protector and Guardian), *Ash-Shakur*
   (The Grateful), *As-Samad* (The Eternal and Self-
   Sufficient), and how we can channel those names
   of Allah in our daily lives.

Let's make dua

1. Originator of the heavens and the earth! You are
   my Guardian in this world and the Hereafter. Allow
   me to die as one who submits and join me with the
   righteous. (12:101)

فَاطِرَ ٱلسَّمَـٰوَٰتِ وَٱلْأَرْضِ أَنتَ وَلِيِّ فِى ٱلدُّنْيَا وَٱلْءَاخِرَةِ تَوَفَّنِى مُسْلِمًا وَأَلْحِقْنِى
بِٱلصَّـٰلِحِينَ

2. The Prophet (s) used to recite this in the morning
   and evening:

   O Allah, I seek Your forgiveness and Your protection
   in this world and the Next. O Allah, I seek Your
   forgiveness and Your protection in my religion,

in my worldly affairs, in my family and in my wealth.
O Allah, conceal my secrets and preserve me from
anguish. O Allah, guard me from what is in front of
me and behind me, from my left, and from my right,
and from above me. I seek refuge in Your Greatness
from being struck down from beneath me. (Bukhari
and others)

اللَّهُمَّ إِنِّي أَسْأَلُكَ الْعَافِيَةَ فِي الدُّنْيَا وَالْآخِرَةِ، اللَّهُمَّ إِنِّي أَسْأَلُكَ الْعَفْوَ وَالْعَافِيَةَ فِي
دِينِي وَدُنْيَايَ وَأَهْلِي وَمَالِي، اللَّهُمَّ اسْتُرْ عَوْرَاتِي وَآمِنْ رَوْعَاتِي، اللَّهُمَّ احْفَظْنِي
مِنْ بَيْنِ يَدَيَّ وَمِنْ خَلْفِي وَعَنْ يَمِينِي وَعَنْ شِمَالِي وَمِنْ فَوْقِي وَأَعُوذُ بِعَظَمَتِكَ
مِنْ أَنْ أُغْتَالَ مِنْ تَحْتِي

3. O Turner of the hearts, make my heart firm upon
    your religion. (Tirmithi)

يا مقلّبَ القلوبِ ثَبِّتْ قلبي على دينِك

Let's teach it

A Scout is Loyal
Suggested Curriculum

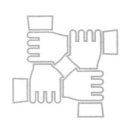

The content included for each characteristic can span several scouting seasons. In this section, we have included a suggested curriculum for an entire month to simplify your planning. On week 4, we assumed the troop or youth group would participate in a campout or outdoor activity. The next section is a blank curriculum for you to design your own.

Week 1: Introduction to Loyal

Open with Quran	3:76 6:152 2:257
Youth Talk	Hadith #2
Leader Talk	• Scout Law definition and Islamic perspective • What does it mean again? • What's in it for me?
Activity	Let's Reflect #1
Closing Dua	Dua #3

Week 2: Loyalty to Justice

Open with Quran	4:135
Youth Talk	Hadith #4
Leader Talk	High and Low Company
Activity	Learning to Lean
Closing Dua	Dua #3

Week 3: Loyalty to Family and Others

Open with Quran	17:24
Youth Talk	Hadith #4
Leader Talk	Loyalty to Khadija
Activity	Let's Reflect #5
Closing Dua	Dua #3

Week 4 Camp: Bringing it All Together

Open with Quran	49:10
Youth Talk	• Hadith #9 • Let's Reflect #9
Leader Talk	
Activity	Gladiator Balloon Battle
Closing Dua	Dua #3 (After each prayer)
Campfire	Let's Reflect #3

Let's teach it

A Scout is Loyal

Design your own Curriculum

Week 1:

Open with Quran	
Youth Talk	
Leader Talk	
Activity	
Closing Dua	

Week 2:

Open with Quran	
Youth Talk	
Leader Talk	
Activity	
Closing Dua	

Week 3:

Open with Quran	
Youth Talk	
Leader Talk	
Activity	
Closing Dua	

Week 4 Camp:

Open with Quran	
Youth Talk	
Leader Talk	
Activity	
Closing Dua	
Campfire	

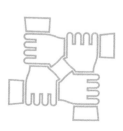

A Scout is Helpful

A Scout is helpful. A Scout cares about other people. A Scout helps others without expecting payment or reward. A Scout fulfills duties to the family by helping at home. A Scout wants the best for everyone and acts to make that happen. A Scout might work for pay, but a Scout does not expect to receive money for being helpful. A Good Turn that is done in the hope of getting a tip or a favor is not a Good Turn at all. (The Scout Handbook)

The Muslim is always in the service of people, helping them with their burdens and relieving their troubles. Islam teaches us to help each other in doing good deeds and to help each other by reminding one another about Allah, while expecting the reward from Allah alone.

Allah is *An-Naseer*, The Helper. *An-Naseer* helps us physically, mentally and emotionally through the small and the big things. We should never lose hope and think that Allah will not come to our aid. Rather, we seek His assistance and strive to help others knowing Allah will help us in return. And when Allah supports us and grants us success, we humble ourselves by praising Him and asking for His forgiveness.

What do Allah and the Prophet (s) say about being helpful?

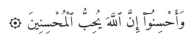

In the Quran

وَأَحْسِنُوٓاْ إِنَّ ٱللَّهَ يُحِبُّ ٱلْمُحْسِنِينَ ۞

... Do good to others, surely Allah loves those who do good to others. (2:195)

وَيَٰقَوْمِ لَآ أَسْـَٔلُكُمْ عَلَيْهِ مَالًا إِنْ أَجْرِىَ إِلَّا عَلَى ٱللَّهِ

And O my people, I asked of you no payment for it, my reward is from none but Allah... (11:29)

وَتَعَاوَنُوا۟ عَلَى ٱلْبِرِّ وَٱلتَّقْوَىٰ وَلَا تَعَاوَنُوا۟ عَلَى ٱلْإِثْمِ وَٱلْعُدْوَٰنِ

...And help one another to do what is right and good; do not help one another towards sin and hostility... (5:2)

يَٰٓأَيُّهَا ٱلَّذِينَ ءَامَنُوٓا۟ إِن تَنصُرُوا۟ ٱللَّهَ يَنصُرْكُمْ وَيُثَبِّتْ أَقْدَامَكُمْ ۞

You who believe! If you help Allah, He will help you and make you stand firm.

وَإِن تَوَلَّوْا۟ فَٱعْلَمُوٓا۟ أَنَّ ٱللَّهَ مَوْلَىٰكُمْ نِعْمَ ٱلْمَوْلَىٰ وَنِعْمَ ٱلنَّصِيرُ ۞

...And if they turn away, then know that Allah is your Protector. What an excellent Protector and what an excellent Helper! (8:40)

1. "If a person relieves a Muslim of his trouble, Allah will relieve him of his troubles on the Day of Resurrection." (Muslim)

2. Aisha was asked how the Prophet (s) spent his time at home. She said, "He used to keep himself busy serving his family and when it was time for the prayer, he would get up for prayer." (Bukhari)

3. "The most beloved people to Allah are those who are most beneficial to people. The most beloved deed to Allah is to make a Muslim happy, to remove one of his troubles, to forgive his debt, or to feed his hunger. That I walk with a brother regarding a need is more beloved to me than secluding myself in this mosque in Madinah for a month. Whoever swallows his anger, then Allah will conceal his faults. Whoever suppresses his anger, even though he is capable of enacting his anger, then Allah will secure his heart on the Day of Resurrection. Whoever walks with his brother regarding a need until he secures it for him, then Allah Almighty will make his footing firm across the Bridge on the Day when the footings are shaken." (Albani)

4. "When Allah wills good for His servant, He uses him." The Companions asked, "How does He use him?" He said, "He guides him to do good deeds before he dies." (Tirmithi)

What does it mean again?

A Muslim cares about others. We are always looking for ways to help and be of benefit to other people, because that is one of the best ways to earn Allah's love.

Pay it forward. Allah helped us and gave us health and resources. We owe it to show gratefulness by helping Allah's creation in moments of need.

A Muslim gives freely without expecting anything in return. The reward for being helpful to others is with Allah, not with people. We should not expect appreciation or compliments.

Helping at home is extremely important. Helping at home often goes unnoticed by other people, but it is one of the greatest ways to practice helpfulness, because it serves our parents and those who sacrificed for us and are closest to us.

Tell Me A Story

• • • Better than Fasting!

Some of the Companions did all the work while the others were fasting. (pg. 212)

• • • Better than *Itikaaf*!

Ibn Abbas remembers a hadith of the Prophet (s). (pg. 212)

• • • The Most Difficult Job

The Prophet (s) chooses the most difficult job while digging the trench. (pg. 213)

• • • Umar Bakes the Bread

Umar helps a poor woman feed her children. (pg. 214)

What's in it for me?

Immense reward from Allah. Helping others brings about tremendous reward and blessings in our daily life.

Helps you live longer. Research has shown that community service volunteers better manage stress and stave off disease and depression. This might be because volunteering alleviates loneliness and enhances our social lives.

Makes us happy. A team of sociologists tracked 2000 people over a five-year period and found that the happiest people volunteered at least 6 hours per month. Helping others gives us a sense of purpose and enhances our identity.

Let's do this

• • • Help Sensors

If we are not paying attention and being intentional, we often miss the best opportunities to gain reward and help others. Don't wait for someone to ask — be on high alert for opportunities to help. What can you do during this campout or meeting to be helpful? Brainstorm with your youth how to put what you learned into action. Ask those in charge (i.e. camp staff, office administrator) how you can help, whether it be picking up trash, cleaning the bathrooms, or helping in other ways.

• • • A Helpful Meal

Cook a meal together and challenge everyone to find a way to help. No one should have idle hands, and no one should stop working until all of the work is completed. Challenge youth to anticipate what needs to be done and be creative in finding ways to help.

• • • Helpful Role Playing

Sometimes we don't help because we are lost for words or shy to offer help. Youth can role-play different situations and rehearse ways to approach people who need help. How do you approach them? Rehearse what

you might say to offer help: What can I do to help you?
Would you like me to clean, carry this, etc.? Some of
these role-play situations may include:

1. A neighbor unloading groceries from her trunk.

2. A mother with a toddler who is throwing a tantrum
   in the airport.

3. An elderly uncle is trying to find a chair to sit on
   during prayer.

4. A new youth or scout seems confused and lonely
   during a youth or troop meeting.

Let's reflect

1. What good turn or deed have you done today? Who has been helpful to you? How did it make you feel?

2. In addition to your friends and family, who can and should you be helpful to? Think of your home environment, inner circle, community, nation, and globally.

3. Helping at home can sometimes be boring or draining. How can we change our mindset toward helping our parents and siblings?

4. Whoever wants to be a leader must first be a servant. What does this mean? How does being helpful grow our leadership?

5. We might come up with excuses of why we shouldn't help in a situation. What are those excuses?

6. What names and attributes of Allah remind us of the importance of being helpful to others? Discuss how Allah is *Al-Muhsin* (The One who Makes Everything Excellent), *Al-Kareem* (The Generous), *An-Nāfi'* (The Beneficent), *An-Naseer* (The Helper) and how we can channel those names of Allah in our daily lives.

Let's make dua

1. O Allah, help us to remember You, to thank You, and to worship You in the best way. (al-Hakim)

اللَّهُمَّ أَعِنَّا عَلَى ذِكْرِكَ وَشُكْرِكَ وَحُسْنِ عِبَادَتِكَ

2. O Allah, guide me to the best of character, for no one can guide to good character except you. And save me from bad character, for no one can save from bad character except You. (Muslim)

اللَّهُمَّ اهْدِنِي لِأَحْسَنِ الْأَخْلَاقِ لَا يَهْدِي لِأَحْسَنِهَا إِلَّا أَنْتَ، وَاصْرِفْ عَنِّي سَيِّئَهَا،
لَا يَصْرِفُ عَنِّي سَيِّئَهَا إِلَّا أَنْتَ

3. O Lord! Help me and do not help others against me, support me and do not support others against me, plan for me and do not plan against me, guide me and make guidance easy for me, and help me against those who wrong me. O Lord! Make me always grateful to You, always remembering You, always in awe of You, obedient, humble and always returning to You. O Lord! Accept my repentance and wash away my sins, answer my supplication, guide my heart, make my tongue speak the truth, make my position firm, and remove resentment from my heart. (Ibn Majah)

رَبِّ أَعِنِّي وَلَا تُعِنْ عَلَيَّ وَانْصُرْنِي وَلَا تَنْصُرْ عَلَيَّ وَامْكُرْ لِي وَلَا تَمْكُرْ عَلَيَّ وَاهْدِنِي
وَيَسِّرِ الْهُدَى لِي وَانْصُرْنِي عَلَى مَنْ بَغَى عَلَيَّ رَبِّ اجْعَلْنِي لَكَ شَكَّارًا لَكَ ذَكَّارًا
لَكَ رَهَّابًا لَكَ مُطِيعًا إِلَيْكَ مُخْبِتًا إِلَيْكَ أَوَّاهًا مُنِيبًا رَبِّ تَقَبَّلْ تَوْبَتِي وَاغْسِلْ حَوْبَتِي
وَأَجِبْ دَعْوَتِي وَاهْدِ قَلْبِي وَسَدِّدْ لِسَانِي وَثَبِّتْ حُجَّتِي وَاسْلُلْ سَخِيمَةَ قَلْبِي

Let's teach it

A Scout is Helpful
Suggested Curriculum

The content included for each characteristic can span several scouting seasons. In this section, we have included a suggested curriculum for an entire month to simplify your planning. On week 4, we assumed the troop or youth group would participate in a campout or outdoor activity. The next section is a blank curriculum for you to design your own.

Week 1: Introduction to Helpful

Open with Quran	2:195 11:29
Youth Talk	Hadith #1
Leader Talk	• Scout Law definition and Islamic perspective • What does it mean again? • What's in it for me?
Activity	
Closing Dua	Dua #1

Week 2: Helping at Home

Open with Quran	5:2
Youth Talk	Hadith #2
Leader Talk	Umar Bakes the Bread
Activity	Helpful Role Playing
Closing Dua	Dua #1

Week 3: Allah is the Best of Helpers

Open with Quran	8:40
Youth Talk	Hadith #3
Leader Talk	Better than *Itikaaf!*
Activity	Let's Reflect #6
Closing Dua	Dua #1

Week 4 Camp: Bringing it All Together

Open with Quran	2:195 11:29
Youth Talk	• Hadith #4 • Let's Reflect #4
Leader Talk	Better than Fasting!
Activity	• Helpful Meal • Help Sensors
Closing Dua	Dua #1 (After each prayer)
Campfire	Let's Reflect #2

Let's teach it

A Scout is Helpful

Design your own Curriculum

Week 1:	
Open with Quran	
Youth Talk	
Leader Talk	
Activity	
Closing Dua	

Week 2:	
Open with Quran	
Youth Talk	
Leader Talk	
Activity	
Closing Dua	

Week 3:

Open with Quran	
Youth Talk	
Leader Talk	
Activity	
Closing Dua	

Week 4 Camp:

Open with Quran	
Youth Talk	
Leader Talk	
Activity	
Closing Dua	
Campfire	

A Scout is Friendly

A Scout is friendly. Be a friend to everyone, even people who are very different from you. A Scout is a friend to all other scouts. A Scout offers friendship to people of all races, religions, and nations, and a Scout respects them even if their beliefs and customs are different. (The Scout Handbook)

Muslims should treat everyone equally and befriend everyone regardless of race and ethnicity. This can be witnessed during the Hajj when all men wear a white cloth regardless of race or status. The Muslim is friendly and neighborly towards people of all religions, respecting their houses of worship and joining hands with them in good causes.

Allah is *Al-Lateef*, the Gentle and Benevolent. He knows our thoughts and emotions and deals with us gently through kind, subtle, and friendly ways. When we recognize how *Al-Lateef* treats us with so much gentleness, that should make us want to be a source of friendliness and kindness to others as a way of being grateful to Him.

What do Allah and the Prophet say about being friendly?

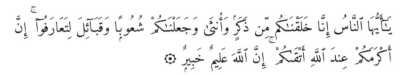

In the Quran

يَٰٓأَيُّهَا ٱلنَّاسُ إِنَّا خَلَقْنَٰكُم مِّن ذَكَرٍ وَأُنثَىٰ وَجَعَلْنَٰكُمْ شُعُوبًا وَقَبَآئِلَ لِتَعَارَفُوٓاْ إِنَّ أَكْرَمَكُمْ عِندَ ٱللَّهِ أَتْقَىٰكُمْ إِنَّ ٱللَّهَ عَلِيمٌ خَبِيرٌ ۝

People, We created you all from a single man and a single woman, and made you into races and tribes so that you should recognize one another. In Allah's eyes, the most honored of you are the ones most mindful of Him: Allah is All-Knowing, All-Aware. (49:13)

وَٱصْبِرْ نَفْسَكَ مَعَ ٱلَّذِينَ يَدْعُونَ رَبَّهُم بِٱلْغَدَوٰةِ وَٱلْعَشِيِّ يُرِيدُونَ وَجْهَهُۥ وَلَا تَعْدُ عَيْنَاكَ عَنْهُمْ تُرِيدُ زِينَةَ ٱلْحَيَوٰةِ ٱلدُّنْيَا

Content yourself with those who pray to their Lord morning and evening, seeking His approval, and do not let your eyes turn away from them out of desire for the attractions of this worldly life... (18:28)

فَبِمَا رَحْمَةٍ مِّنَ ٱللَّهِ لِنتَ لَهُمْ وَلَوْ كُنتَ فَظًّا غَلِيظَ ٱلْقَلْبِ لَٱنفَضُّواْ مِنْ حَوْلِكَ

By an act of mercy from Allah, you [Prophet] were gentle in your dealings with them—had you been harsh, or hard-hearted, they would have dispersed and left you—so pardon them and ask forgiveness for them. (3:159)

إِنَّمَا الْمُؤْمِنُونَ إِخْوَةٌ فَأَصْلِحُوا بَيْنَ أَخَوَيْكُمْ ۚ وَاتَّقُوا اللَّهَ لَعَلَّكُمْ تُرْحَمُونَ ۝

The believers are brothers, so make peace between your two brothers and be mindful of Allah, so that you may be given mercy. (49:10)

يَا وَيْلَتَىٰ لَيْتَنِي لَمْ أَتَّخِذْ فُلَانًا خَلِيلًا ۝

Woe to me! I wish I had never taken so-and-so as a close friend. (25:28)

In the Hadith

1. "There is no superiority of an Arab over a non-Arab, nor of a non-Arab over an Arab, and no superiority of a white person over a black person, nor of a black person over a white person, except on the basis of *taqwa* [God-mindfulness]. All are from Adam, and Adam is from dust." (Ahmad)

2. "Allah Almighty said: My love is a right upon those who befriend each other for My sake. My love is a right upon those who remain connected for My sake. My love is a right upon those who visit each other for My sake. And My love is a right upon those who sacrifice for each other for My sake." (Al-Albani)

3. "When you smile in the face of your brother, it is charity..." (Tirmithi)

4. "Being kind and friendly to people is a charity." (Ibn Hibban)

5. "The believer is friendly and befriended, for there is no goodness in one who is neither friendly nor befriended. The best of people are those who are most beneficial to people." (al-Albani)

6. The Messenger of Allah (s) would meet even the worst people with eye contact and speak at their level, by which he would show friendliness to them. He would meet me with eye contact and speak at my level, until I thought that I was the best of people. (Tirmithi)

7. "None of you truly believes until he loves for his brother what he loves for himself." (Bukhari & Muslim)

8. "The example of a good companion and a bad companion is like that of the seller of musk and the blacksmith. So as for the seller of musk then either he will grant you some, or you buy some from him, or at least you enjoy a pleasant smell from him. As for the one who blows the blacksmith's bellows then either he will burn your clothes or you will get an offensive smell from him." (Bukhari & Muslim)

9. "The Muslim is a brother to another Muslim. He does not wrong him, nor surrender him. Whoever fulfills the needs of his brother, Allah will fulfill his needs. Whoever relieves a Muslim from distress, Allah will relieve him from distress on the Day of Resurrection. Whoever covers the faults of a Muslim, Allah will cover his faults on the Day of Resurrection." (Bukhari & Muslim)

What does it mean again?

A Muslim is friendly with everyone. A Muslim is neither rude nor disrespectful towards others. He or she gets to know others and behaves in the best possible manner towards everyone, regardless of faith, race and ethnicity.

Initiate friendships! Go out of your way to make friends with people who are different from you and who are not in your clique.

Muslims have a special bond. In Islam, that special bond is one of brotherhood and sisterhood based on faith, good character, and treating others the way they want to be treated. True friends keep us attached to Allah and His religion.

Tell Me A Story

• • • **Three Best Friends**

Three friends do their best to help each other with surprising results. (pg. 216)

• • • **The Traveling Friend**

Allah sent an angel to ask what his motives were. (pg. 218)

• • • **Abu Bakr, True Friend and Supporter**

No friend like Abu Bakr. (pg. 219)

What's in it for me?

Safe from the Hellfire. The Prophet (s) taught us that the Hellfire is forbidden to touch a person who is polite and kind-natured.

Sound heart, improved mood and reduced tension. Having a friendly attitude towards others keeps you at peace with yourself.

Diversity of ideas. Being open to others from different backgrounds leads to different ideas.

Support through tough times. Good friends help you cope through challenges you may face in life. They may help you study for a difficult exam, cope with a loss of a loved one or solve problems you encounter.

Helps you stay on track. A good friend will encourage you to do good deeds, give you good advice, and keep you from doing wrong.

Let's do this

• • • Not So Friendly Feelings

This is an activity to help youth empathize with those who may not have as many friends. Distribute index cards to the group. As you read out each scenario below, each group should write down expressions describing how a person might feel in each situation and add them to the container. After each question, read the responses and discuss. Example of scenarios:

1. Being the last to be chosen for a team.

2. Not finding a partner for a classroom activity.

3. You see your friend but he is busy, doesn't smile, and doesn't seem to notice you.

4. Telling a joke or doing a stunt and no one laughs or seems interested.

5. Sitting in the mosque gym where a lot of kids are playing but no one invites you to join their game.

6. Saying *salaam* but no one responds.

(*Supplies: Index cards, container to hold the index cards*)

• • • Speed Chatting

Make a list of a few prompts and opening lines you can use to strike up a conversation with a stranger or new friend. The goal is to develop skill in striking conversation with someone they don't know. Set a timer for 90 seconds, have youth match up with a random partner, announce the opening line, and have them talk to each other for 90 seconds. Do several rounds of the activity, with a different prompt each time, and then discuss. What made the interactions easier or harder? What topics were difficult to talk about? Did anyone observe some extra friendly gestures? Unfriendly gestures? Troubleshoot any difficulties in a cooperative and friendly manner. Some conversation starters:

- Start with a compliment.

- Start with something obvious you have in common.

- What movies do you like?

- What brought you here today?

- What did you think of lunch/snack today?

● ● ● Control Tower Friend

Play the Control Tower game which sees one member of the group blindfolded and their partner guiding them through an obstacle course. When they have successfully reached the end of the course, roles are swapped, and the course changed. This is very good for establishing communication and friendship, as well as creating a fun and competitive atmosphere. Be sure to pair youth up with others they don't know as well. Play again with someone they know very well. Debrief on the different experiences.

• • • Whodunit?

On an index card, have everyone jot down something interesting he or she has done. Gather the cards, shuffle and then distribute to the participants. Each person reads aloud their card, and the group guesses who did it. The guessed person simply answers "Yes" or "No." If the guess is correct, the guessed person may briefly explain her experience. Debrief with participants by asking how knowing a person helps you be more friendly. (*Supplies: index cards, pens*)

Source: The Classroom

Read more at *https://masnational.org/diversity*

• • • Create a World Map

Spend time creating a world map that explores the family origins of each youth. Have each youth research the following:

- Where did their family come from?
- What is their native language?
- What food did they enjoy?
- What was life like in their native land?

Source: Sign Up Genius

Read more at *https://masnational.org/diversityactivity*

Let's reflect

1. Reflect on your friends and those you hang out with. Do you have a diverse group of friends from different ethnicities and socio-economic backgrounds? Why or why not?

2. What are some positive characteristics of good friends? Bad friends?

3. Is it better to be alone or to mix with the people? Explain.

4. In your opinion, what tears apart friendships? Explain.

5. Name some practical actions you can do to be friendly to all.

6. What is the difference between acquaintances, friends, and true friends?

7. When might you feel uncomfortable befriending someone? Explain.

8. What names and attributes of Allah remind us of the importance of being friendly to others? Discuss how Allah is *Al-Lateef* (The Gentle and Friendly), *Al-Waali* (The Protector), *Al-Waliy* (The Guardian), *An-Naseer* (The Helpful) and how we can channel those names of Allah in our daily lives.

Let's make dua

1. O Allah! Bring our hearts together, reconcile our differences, guide us to the ways of peace, take us out of darkness into light, and keep us away from sins, the apparent and the hidden. (Abu Dawud)

اللّهُمَّ أَلِّفْ بَيْنَ قُلُوبِنَا وَأَصْلِحْ ذَاتَ بَيْنِنَا وَاهْدِنَا سُبُلَ السَّلاَمَ وَنَجِّنَا مِنَ الظُّلُمَاتِ إِلَى النُّورِ وَجَنِّبْنَا الْفَوَاحِشَ مَا ظَهَرَ مِنْهَا وَمَا بَطَنَ

2. O Allah, I ask You for Your love and the love of those who love You, and love for the actions that will lead me to Your love. (Tirmithi)

اللّهُمَّ إِنِّي أَسْأَلُكَ حُبَّكَ وَحُبَّ مَنْ يُحِبُّكَ وَالْعَمَلَ الَّذِي يُبَلِّغُنِي حُبَّكَ

Let's teach it

A Scout is Friendly
Suggested Curriculum

The content included for each characteristic can span several scouting seasons. In this section, we have included a suggested curriculum for an entire month to simplify your planning. On week 4, we assumed the troop or youth group would participate in a campout or outdoor activity. The next section is a blank curriculum for you to design your own.

Week 1: Introduction to Friendly

Open with Quran	49:13 18:28
Youth Talk	Hadith #2
Leader Talk	• Scout Law definition and Islamic perspective • What does it mean again? • What's in it for me?
Activity	
Closing Dua	Dua #1

Week 2: Friendly to all

Open with Quran	49:13
Youth Talk	Hadith #1
Leader Talk	Hadith #8
Activity	Create a World Map
Closing Dua	Dua #1

Week 3: True Friendship

Open with Quran	3:159
Youth Talk	Hadith #9
Leader Talk	Abu Bakr, True Friend and Supporter
Activity	Control Tower Friend
Closing Dua	Dua #1

Week 4: Bringing it All Together

Open with Quran	49:13 3:159
Youth Talk	• Hadith #3, 4 • Let's Reflect #8
Leader Talk	Three Best Friends
Activity	Whodunit?
Closing Dua	Dua #1 (After each prayer)
Campfire	Let's Reflect #1, 2, 3, 4

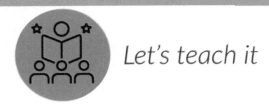

Let's teach it

A Scout is Friendly

Design your own Curriculum

Week 1:

Open with Quran	
Youth Talk	
Leader Talk	
Activity	
Closing Dua	

Week 2:

Open with Quran	
Youth Talk	
Leader Talk	
Activity	
Closing Dua	

Week 3:

Open with Quran	
Youth Talk	
Leader Talk	
Activity	
Closing Dua	

Week 4:

Open with Quran	
Youth Talk	
Leader Talk	
Activity	
Closing Dua	
Campfire	

A Scout is Courteous

A Scout is courteous. A Scout is polite to people of all ages and positions. A Scout understands that using good manners makes it easier for people to get along. Being courteous shows that you are aware of the feelings of others. The habits of courtesy that you practice as a Scout will stay with you throughout your life.
(The Scout Handbook)

The Prophet (s) teaches us that he was sent to perfect good moral character. As he is our role model, we aim to follow his practice and demonstrate his gentle and polite demeanor with others. He (s) took great care in ensuring those he interacted with felt his love and care.

Allah is *Al-Haleem*, The Forbearing. He is tolerant and gentle with us, giving us many second chances even when we make mistakes and disobey Him. Allah is also *As-Salaam*, the Source of peace and safety. We seek peace and security from Allah which enables us to be at peace with others. When we greet each other with *assalaamu alaikum*, it is as if we are saying, "I place you in the security of God's name, *As-Salaam*.

What do Allah and the Prophet (s) say about being courteous?

In the Quran

فَبِمَا رَحْمَةٍ مِّنَ ٱللَّهِ لِنتَ لَهُمْ ۖ وَلَوْ كُنتَ فَظًّا غَلِيظَ ٱلْقَلْبِ لَٱنفَضُّوا۟ مِنْ حَوْلِكَ

By an act of mercy from Allah, you [Prophet] were gentle in your dealings with them. Had you been harsh, or hard-hearted, they would have dispersed and left you... (3:159)

يَـٰٓأَيُّهَا ٱلَّذِينَ ءَامَنُوا۟ لَا يَسْخَرْ قَوْمٌ مِّن قَوْمٍ عَسَىٰٓ أَن يَكُونُوا۟ خَيْرًا مِّنْهُمْ وَلَا نِسَآءٌ مِّن نِّسَآءٍ عَسَىٰٓ أَن يَكُنَّ خَيْرًا مِّنْهُنَّ ۖ وَلَا تَلْمِزُوٓا۟ أَنفُسَكُمْ وَلَا تَنَابَزُوا۟ بِٱلْأَلْقَـٰبِ

O believers! Do not let some men ridicule others, they may be better than them, nor let some women ridicule other women, they may be better than them. Do not defame one another, nor call each other by offensive nicknames... (49:11)

وَقَضَىٰ رَبُّكَ أَلَّا تَعْبُدُوٓا۟ إِلَّآ إِيَّاهُ وَبِٱلْوَٰلِدَيْنِ إِحْسَـٰنًا ۚ إِمَّا يَبْلُغَنَّ عِندَكَ ٱلْكِبَرَ أَحَدُهُمَآ أَوْ كِلَاهُمَا فَلَا تَقُل لَّهُمَآ أُفٍّ وَلَا تَنْهَرْهُمَا وَقُل لَّهُمَا قَوْلًا كَرِيمًا ۝

For your Lord has decreed that you worship none but Him. And honor your parents. If one or both of them reach old age in your care, never say to them [even] 'ugh,' nor yell at them. Rather, address them respectfully. (17:23)

يَٰٓأَيُّهَا ٱلَّذِينَ ءَامَنُوٓا۟ إِذَا قِيلَ لَكُمْ تَفَسَّحُوا۟ فِى ٱلْمَجَٰلِسِ فَٱفْسَحُوا۟ يَفْسَحِ ٱللَّهُ لَكُمْ

O you who have attained faith, when you are told, "Make room for one another in assemblies," then make room so that Allah makes room for you... (58:11)

يَٰٓأَيُّهَا ٱلَّذِينَ ءَامَنُوا۟ لِيَسْتَـٔذِنكُمُ ٱلَّذِينَ مَلَكَتْ أَيْمَٰنُكُمْ وَٱلَّذِينَ لَمْ يَبْلُغُوا۟ ٱلْحُلُمَ مِنكُمْ ثَلَٰثَ مَرَّٰتٍ مِّن قَبْلِ صَلَوٰةِ ٱلْفَجْرِ وَحِينَ تَضَعُونَ ثِيَابَكُم مِّنَ ٱلظَّهِيرَةِ وَمِنۢ بَعْدِ صَلَوٰةِ ٱلْعِشَآءِ ثَلَٰثُ عَوْرَٰتٍ لَّكُمْ

O you who have attained faith, let those whom you rightfully possess and those of you who have not reached puberty seek your permission (before entering) on three occasions: before the dawn prayer and at noon when you lay aside your clothes and after the evening prayer—three occasions of privacy for you... (24:58)

فَإِن لَّمْ تَجِدُوا۟ فِيهَآ أَحَدًا فَلَا تَدْخُلُوهَا حَتَّىٰ يُؤْذَنَ لَكُمْ ۖ وَإِن قِيلَ لَكُمُ ٱرْجِعُوا۟ فَٱرْجِعُوا۟ ۖ هُوَ أَزْكَىٰ لَكُمْ ۚ وَٱللَّهُ بِمَا تَعْمَلُونَ عَلِيمٌ ۝

If you find no one at home, do not enter it until you have been given permission. And if you are asked to leave, then leave. That is purer for you. And Allah has perfect knowledge of what you do. (24:28)

• • • In the Hadith

1. "Verily, the believer may reach by his good character the rank of one who regularly fasts and stands for prayer at night." (Abu Dawud)

2. Abu Hurairah said, "I heard Abu al-Qasim (the Prophet), upon him be peace, say, 'The best among you in Islam are those with the best character, so long as they develop a sense of understanding.'" (Ahmad)

3. "The Muslim is the one from whose tongue and hand the people are safe." (Agreed upon)

4. "Shall I not tell you for whom the Hellfire is forbidden? For every person who is approachable, courteous, tender, and easygoing." (Tirmithi)

5. "Every joint of a person must perform a charity each day that the sun rises: to judge justly between two people is charity. To help a man with his mount, lifting him onto it or hoisting up his belongings onto it, is charity. The good word is charity. Every step that you take toward the prayer is charity, and removing a harmful object from the way is charity." (Bukhari, Muslim)

6. "...Angels are offended by the same things that offend people." (Muslim)

7. A man asked the Prophet (s): "O Allah's messenger, should I ask permission from my mother to enter her room?" The Prophet said "Yes." The man continued, "But Allah's messenger, she lives in my home." The

Prophet (s) said, "Ask her permission." The man said, "But I am the one caring for her!" The Prophet said, "Ask her permission. Would you like it if you saw her unclothed?" "No!" the man replied. The Prophet (s) said, "Then, ask for her permission." (Ibn Hajar)

8. When the Prophet (s) used to approach and knock on someone's door, he would not stand facing the door directly, but would face to the right or left of the door and he would say, "*Assalamu Alaikum, Assalamu Alaikum.*" (Abu Dawud)

9. "Ask permission to enter [a house] three times. Enter if you are given permission, otherwise, leave." (Bukhari, Muslim)

Politeness knows no age. All ages should learn to be polite, and everyone deserves to be treated with courtesy, whether young or old. The Prophet (s) said, "Whoever is not kind to the younger ones or does not respect the elders is not from my nation." (Ahmad)

Empathy with others. The Prophet (s) said, "The believers in their mutual kindness, compassion and sympathy are just like one body. When one of the limbs suffers, the whole body responds to it with wakefulness and fever." (Bukhari)

Politeness requires intentionality. Opportunities to demonstrate politeness will pass you by if you are inattentive to your surroundings and to the people around you.

Tell Me A Story

Immense reward. Abu Hurairah said that the Prophet (s) said, "If one has good manners, one may attain the same level of merit as those who spend their nights in prayer." (Ahmad)

Being close to the Prophet (s) in the Hereafter. Jabir ibn Abdallah reported that the Prophet (s) said, "The most beloved and nearest to my gathering on the Day of Resurrection are those of you with the best character. The most reprehensible of you and the furthest from my gathering on the Day of Resurrection will be the pompous, extravagant, and pretentious." (Tirmithi)

Better family relationships. We all know it's more difficult to be polite around family, but the reward from Allah is immense, not to mention the love that it fosters between family members.

By being courteous, your friendships will flourish and you will be more sought out. People want to work with others who are polite and courteous.

Don't miss out. Abdallah ibn 'Amr said, "There are four characteristics that, if one has them, he will never be deprived in this life. They are: good character, pure provision, honesty, and trustworthiness."

Self-esteem boost. One small gesture or offer of help can make a difference in someone's life which boosts your self-esteem and gives you immense personal satisfaction.

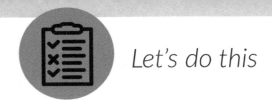

Let's do this

• • • Phone Stacking Game

Have your youth sit in a circle or at a table and have them put their cell phones in the middle. At the beginning of the meal, everyone puts their phone face down at the center of the table. As time goes on, you'll hear various calls, texts, and emails, but you can't pick up your phone. If you're the first one to give in to temptation, you're buying dinner for everyone else. If no one picks up, then everyone pays for themselves.

• • • Manner Charades

First, a brainstorming session! As a patrol or youth group, quickly spend a few minutes noting down some actions that demonstrate good and bad manners on separate pieces of paper. Next, fold the pieces of paper, place in a hat and mix them up. Take turns choosing a piece of paper from the hat and act out the scenario described. The youth, in turn, must reveal if they think the action is good or bad. Then they must state what they believe the action to be! (*Supplies: strips of paper, pencils, hat*)

• • • Etiquette Role Play

You can write several etiquette scenarios on strips of paper that explore matters such as:

1. How to pass an item

2. How to introduce someone new

3. What to do when you accidentally bump into someone

4. How to give a compliment

5. Offer a seat to someone elderly or a mother who is pregnant or with kids

Place the scenarios in a hat and shake them up. Divide youth into pairs. Have each pair pick a scenario out of the hat and then give the pairs a few minutes to discuss their scenario. Let each pair have a turn to act out their scenario for others. (*Supplies: strips of paper, hat*)

• • • Telephone Manners Game

Teach your youth how to properly ask for someone over the phone. Explain that they must first say hello or *salaam*, identify themselves and ask for the person they would like to speak to. For example, one would say, "*Assalamu alaikum*, this is Ahmed. How are you? May I please speak to Tariq?" Divide your youth into threes. The first person will be the caller, the second person will be the parent and the last person will be the caller's friend. Have the caller use a cell phone to call the parent's home and properly ask for his friend. Debrief by asking: What makes it difficult to speak on the phone with an adult you may not know? What can you do to make it less uncomfortable?

• • • Receiving Gifts Game

Familiarize the patrol or youth group with the proper way to show appreciation for a gift they've received. Have group members wrap inexpensive gifts or random items such as socks, coffee mugs, or dental floss, and put their name on it. Place all the gifts in a large pile. Have each person pick a different gift from the pile and open the gift. Regardless of whether they like the gift, they must still show appreciation to the giver. Tell them to go over to the one who brought their gifts and say, "Thank you. I really appreciate it."

Let's reflect

1. The Prophet (s) was always the first to greet another and would not withdraw his hand from a handshake till the other man withdrew his. If one wanted to say something to him, he would not turn away until the other had finished. What type of impression does this level of attentiveness leave on people's minds?

2. Share examples of people in your life who have been courteous and left a lasting impression on you.

3. Is it challenging to be courteous? Why or why not? How does being mindful and conscious help us be more courteous versus just relying on our habits?

4. A Harvard study showed that people on average touched their phone once every 3 minutes. How does that make it difficult to be courteous? According to research, those who text excessively each day show a decrease in reflective thought, which can be related to the ability to be courteous. Evaluate how technology may interfere with being courteous.

5. What are some ways that people act rude? What rude things bother you most?

6. Some things that don't seem rude to me seem rude to others. In order to be courteous to my parents, should I express courtesy according to what seems courteous to me, or what seems courteous to them?

7. The word "sucks" is currently defined as "to be objectionable or inadequate." (Merriam-Webster Dictionary) Yet, it used to have a very different meaning, so offensive that women voted it as the swear word that most offended them. For this reason, most journalists won't use it. Many people still remember the word's perverse meaning, and that's why it's offensive to them. How does this understanding impact the way we can be polite toward older people?

8. What names and attributes of Allah remind us of the importance of being courteous to others? Discuss how Allah is As-Salaam (The Source of Peace and Safety) and Al-Haleem (The Forbearing) and how we can channel these names of Allah in our daily lives.

Let's make dua

1. O Allah, guide me to the best of character, for no one can guide to good character except You. And save me from bad character, for no one can save from bad character except You. (Muslim)

اللَّهُمَّ اهْدِنِي لأَحْسَنِ الأَخْلَاقِ لا يهْدِي لأَحْسَنِهَا إلَّا أنْتَ، واصرِفْ عَنِّي سَيِّئَهَا، لَا يَصْرِفُ عَنِّي سَيِّئَهَا إلَّا أنْتَ

2. O Allah, I ask You for good health, chastity, trustworthiness, good manners and to be content with destiny. (Bukhari)

اللَّهُمَّ إنِّي أَسْألُكَ الصِّحَّةَ والْعِفَّةَ والأَمَانَةَ وحُسْنَ الْخُلُقِ والرِّضَا بِالْقَدَرِ

3. O Allah! I seek refuge in You from reprehensible manners, deeds and whims. (Tirmithi)

اللَّهُمَّ إنِّي أَعُوذُ بِكَ مِنْ مُنْكَرَاتِ الأَخْلَاقِ والأَعْمَالِ والأَهْوَاءِ

4. O Allah, You are As-Salaam (Peace), From You is all peace, blessed are You, Possessor of majesty and honor. (Muslim)

اللَّهُمَّ أنْتَ السَّلَامُ ومِنْكَ السَّلَامُ تَبَارَكْتَ يا ذا الجَلَالِ والإِكْرَام

Let's teach it

A Scout is Courteous

Suggested Curriculum

The content included for each characteristic can span several scouting seasons. In this section, we have included a suggested curriculum for an entire month to simplify your planning. On week 4, we assumed the troop or youth group would participate in a campout or outdoor activity. The next section is a blank curriculum for you to design your own.

Week 1: Introduction to Courteous

Open with Quran	3:15
Youth Talk	• Hadith #1 • A Mistake in the Mosque
Leader Talk	• Scout Law definition and Islamic perspective • What does it mean again? • What's in it for me?
Closing Dua	Dua #3

Week 2: Common Courtesy

Open with Quran	58:11, 24:28, 24:58, 17:23
Youth Talk	Hadith #5
Leader Talk	Two Brothers' Creativity
Activity	Telephone Manners Game
Closing Dua	Dua #3

Week 3: Being Courteous when its hard

Open with Quran	49:11
Youth Talk	Hadith #3
Leader Talk	Courtesy in the Face of Rudeness
Activity	
Closing Dua	Dua #3

Week 4 Camp: Bringing it All Together

Open with Quran	3:15
Youth Talk	Hadith #4
Leader Talk	Let's Reflect #8
Activity	Manner Charades
Closing Dua	Dua #3 (After each prayer)
Campfire	Let's Reflect #1-3

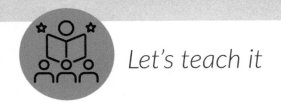

Let's teach it

A Scout is Courteous

Design your own Curriculum

Week 1:

Open with Quran	
Youth Talk	
Leader Talk	
Activity	
Closing Dua	

Week 2:

Open with Quran	
Youth Talk	
Leader Talk	
Activity	
Closing Dua	

Week 3:

Open with Quran	
Youth Talk	
Leader Talk	
Activity	
Closing Dua	

Week 4 Camp:

Open with Quran	
Youth Talk	
Leader Talk	
Activity	
Closing Dua	
Campfire	

A Scout is Kind

A Scout is kind. Scouts treat others as they want others to treat them. A Scout knows there is strength in being gentle. A Scout does not harm or kill any living thing without good reason. Kindness is a sign of true strength. To be kind, you must look beyond yourself and try to understand the needs of others. Take time to listen to people and imagine being in their place. Extending kindness to those around you and having compassion for all people is a powerful agent of change to a more peaceful world. (The Scout Handbook)

The Muslim is gentle with people and other living things. Islam teaches us to be approachable and considerate of others' feelings rather than harsh and stern.

Allah is *Ar-Ra'oof* (The Most Gentle) and *Ar-Rafeeq* (The Most Kind). He deals with us in a gentle and tender fashion. Allah is lenient towards His creations, and He gives us ample opportunity to turn to Him and change our ways. Allah is not harsh and impatient with us; thus, we also should be kind, tolerant and patient with others.

What do Allah and the Prophet (s) say about being kind?

• • • • • In the Quran

إِنَّ ٱللَّهَ بِٱلنَّاسِ لَرَءُوفٌ رَّحِيمٌ ۞

...Verily, Allah is kind and merciful to the people. (2:143)

وَقَضَىٰ رَبُّكَ أَلَّا تَعْبُدُوٓا۟ إِلَّآ إِيَّاهُ وَبِٱلْوَٰلِدَيْنِ إِحْسَٰنًا إِمَّا يَبْلُغَنَّ عِندَكَ ٱلْكِبَرَ
أَحَدُهُمَآ أَوْ كِلَاهُمَا فَلَا تَقُل لَّهُمَآ أُفٍّ وَلَا تَنْهَرْهُمَا وَقُل لَّهُمَا قَوْلًا كَرِيمًا ۞

Your Lord has commanded that you should worship none but Him, and that you be kind to your parents. If either or both of them reach old age with you, say no word that shows impatience with them, and do not be harsh with them, but speak to them respectfully. (17:23)

فَوَيْلٌ لِّلْمُصَلِّينَ ۞ ٱلَّذِينَ هُمْ عَن صَلَاتِهِمْ سَاهُونَ ۞ ٱلَّذِينَ هُمْ يُرَآءُونَ ۞
وَيَمْنَعُونَ ٱلْمَاعُونَ ۞

Woe to those who pray, who are heedless of their prayer, who pray to be seen and withhold small acts of kindness. (107:4-7)

قَوْلٌ مَّعْرُوفٌ وَمَغْفِرَةٌ خَيْرٌ مِّن صَدَقَةٍ يَتْبَعُهَآ أَذًى

Kind words and forgiveness are better than charity followed by injury... (2:263)

فَقُولَا لَهُۥ قَوْلًا لَّيِّنًا لَّعَلَّهُۥ يَتَذَكَّرُ أَوْ يَخْشَىٰ ۞

Speak to [Pharaoh] gently, so perhaps he may be mindful or fearful. (20:44)

• • • In the Hadith

1. "Whoever wishes to be saved from Hell and admitted into Paradise, they should believe in Allah and the Last Day and treat other people the way they themselves would like to be treated." (Muslim)

2. "Whoever is kind, affable, and easy-going, Allah will forbid him from entering Hellfire." (Albani)

3. "Every act of kindness is charity." (Bukhari)

4. "Allah grants for gentleness what he does not grant for harshness. And if Allah loves someone, He gives them gentleness. Any household that is deprived of gentleness is deprived of goodness." (Muslim)

5. "He who is deprived of kindness is deprived of all goodness." (Muslim)

6. Aisha reported that the Messenger of Allah said, "The best of you are the best to their families, and I am the best to my family." (Sunan al-Tirmidhī 3895)

7. Aisha reported: "I was upon a camel that was mis-behaving so I began to strike it. The Messenger of Allah said: 'Aisha, be gentle. Verily, gentleness is not in anything except that it beautifies it, and it is not removed from anything except that it disgraces it.'" (Muslim)

8. The Companions asked, "Is there a reward in being kind even to animals?" The Prophet (s) responded, "In serving any living creature there is reward." (Bukhari & Muslim)

What does it mean again?

We treat others as we want to be treated. We should be kind, approachable, and considerate of others' feelings.

We are kind to all living things. Even plants, animals, and insects deserve our kindness. We should never harm or torment any living thing.

Being gentle is a sign of strong character. Allah loves those who are gentle. The people most deserving of our kindness include those closest to us: our family and siblings.

 Tell Me A Story

● ● ● **Oops, I forgot!**

Anas forgets to do an errand for the Prophet (s). (pg. 226)

● ● ● **True Value**

The Prophet (s) brightens the day of one of his Companions. (pg. 227)

● ● ● **Distressed Creatures**

The Companions find a nest of baby birds. (pg. 228)

• • • A Thirsty Dog

A man uses his shoe to help a thirsty dog. (pg. 228)

• • • Muawiyah's Prayer Mistake

Muawiyah sneezes in the prayer and is not sure what to do. (pg. 229)

What's in it for me?

Kindness is your ticket to Paradise. Hellfire is forbidden to those who are kind and good-natured as our Prophet (s) advised.

People will love you. Luqman is attributed as once saying to his son, "My son, let your speech be good and your face be smiling. You will be more loved by the people than those who give them things." (Ibn Kathir)

Being kind feels good and brings about good. Being kind releases endorphins which improve your mood and make you feel energetic. It brings about so many sources of good, as the Prophet (s) said, "He who is deprived of kindness is deprived of all goodness." (Muslim)

Kindness to family expands your provision and extends your life. The Prophet (s) said, "Whoever is pleased to have his provision expanded and his life span extended, then he should keep good relations with his family." (Bukhari)

Let's do this

• • • T.H.I.N.K

Introduce this acronym for deciding whether something is worth saying or not. "T.H.I.N.K." means before you say anything, you should ask yourself if what you're about to say is: T- True, H- Helpful, I- Inspiring, N- Necessary, K- Kind. Explain T.H.I.N.K before you speak and have scouts practice and remind each other during a campout.

Source: Big Life Journal

• • • Intentionally Kind

For an entire troop or youth meeting, be intentional about being kind. Everyone should perform a random act of kindness whether it be a smile, saying *salaam*, opening the door for someone, assisting someone with a task, etc. At the end of the meeting, have youth share their random act of kindness with their patrol or group and how it made them feel. Be sure to remind the recipient of the act to say "Thank you."

• • • Colors of the Heart

Give the youth some jars of water and some dark food coloring (black or brown). Instruct them to add a drop into the water and imagine the drop was an unkind deed. What did the unkind deed do to the heart (the water)? Ask the youth to brainstorm what can be done to remove the stain from the heart. Finish the activity by adding some bleach to the jar. Talk about how good deeds and kind words, when they follow a bad deed, can erase a bad deed. Share the verse 11:114 "Surely good deeds wipe out evil deeds." (*Supplies: jars of water, dark food coloring, bleach and pipette*)

Source: Let the Little Children Come

Read more at *https://masnational.org/eva*

● ● ●

Words Matter

Pass around squares of sandpaper and pieces of cotton. Ask the youth to describe what each feels like. Point out that words can feel the same way: soft and gentle or sharp and scratchy. Give examples of types of statements, tones, and attitudes that can feel either like cotton or sandpaper. (*Supplies: squares of sandpaper, cotton balls*)

Source: The School Counselor Kind Blog

● ● ● What Comes Out, Stays Out

Offer a tube of toothpaste to the youth and invite them to squeeze out all of the contents. When they are done, ask them to put the toothpaste back in the tube. When they decide it is too hard, discuss how the exercise was like the words we say. Once we say certain words, it is sometimes impossible to take them back. (*Supplies: tubes of toothpaste*)

Let's reflect

1. What was the last act of kindness that you received? How did it make you feel?

2. Think of an act of kindness done inside your house. Maybe you helped your little sister get ready for school. How can this one small act lead to other acts of kindness throughout the day and beyond?

3. When might it be challenging to be kind? For example, in times of crisis, when people can't do anything in return, during disagreements or mistakes, or when you're just in a bad mood. How might you teach yourself to be kind even in these situations?

4. What is the difference between being kind and just being nice?

5. Why is it important to be kind to yourself? What might that look like?

6. Brainstorm ways you can be kind in different areas of your life: with your siblings, with your parents, at school, with your friends, with neighbors, with strangers, and with people you don't like.

7. How is Allah kind to us? What names and attributes of Allah remind us of the importance of being kind? Discuss how Allah is *Ar-Ra'oof* (The Most Gentle)

and *Ar-Rafeeq* (The Most Kind), *Al-Muhsin* (The One who Makes Everything Excellent), *Al-Kareem* (The Generous), *Al-Lateef* (The Kind, the Subtle), and how we can channel those names of Allah in our daily lives.

 ## *Let's make dua*

1. Our Lord, forgive us and our brothers who preceded us in faith and put not in our hearts [any] resentment toward those who have believed. Our Lord, indeed You are Kind and Merciful. (59:10)

رَبَّنَا ٱغْفِرْ لَنَا وَلِإِخْوَٰنِنَا ٱلَّذِينَ سَبَقُونَا بِٱلْإِيمَٰنِ وَلَا تَجْعَلْ فِى قُلُوبِنَا غِلًّا لِّلَّذِينَ ءَامَنُوا۟ رَبَّنَآ إِنَّكَ رَءُوفٌ رَّحِيمٌ

2. O Allah! As You have perfected my form, so perfect my character.

اَللَّهُمَّ كَمَا حَسَّنْتَ خَلْقِي فَحَسِّنْ خُلُقِي

Let's teach it

A Scout is Kind
Suggested Curriculum

The content included for each characteristic can span several scouting seasons. In this section, we have included a suggested curriculum for an entire month to simplify your planning. On week 4, we assumed the troop or youth group would participate in a campout or outdoor activity. The next section is a blank curriculum for you to design your own.

Week 1: Introduction to Kindness

Open with Quran	2:143 107:4-7
Youth Talk	Hadith #1, 2
Leader Talk	• Scout Law definition and Islamic perspective • What does it mean again? • What's in it for me?
Closing Dua	Dua #1

Week 2: Kindness to Family

Open with Quran	17:23
Youth Talk	Hadith #6 and Introduce THINK acronym
Leader Talk	Oops, I forgot!
Activity	What Comes Out, Stays Out
Closing Dua	Dua #1

Week 3: Kindness to Animals

Open with Quran	2:263 20:44
Youth Talk	Hadith #7, 8
Leader Talk	Distressed Creatures
Closing Dua	Dua #1

Week 4 Camp: Bringing it All Together

Open with Quran	2:143 107:4-7
Youth Talk	• Let's Reflect #4 • Hadith #4
Leader Talk	True Value
Activity	Colors of the Heart
Closing Dua	Dua #1 (After each prayer)
Campfire	Let's Reflect #1, 3

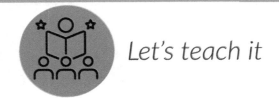

Let's teach it

A Scout is Kind

Design your own Curriculum

Week 1:	
Open with Quran	
Youth Talk	
Leader Talk	
Activity	
Closing Dua	

Week 2:	
Open with Quran	
Youth Talk	
Leader Talk	
Activity	
Closing Dua	

Week 3:

Open with Quran	
Youth Talk	
Leader Talk	
Activity	
Closing Dua	

Week 4 Camp:

Open with Quran	
Youth Talk	
Leader Talk	
Activity	
Closing Dua	
Campfire	

A Scout is Obedient

A Scout is obedient. A Scout follows the rules of the family, school, and troop. Scouts obey the laws of their communities and countries. If a Scout thinks these rules and laws are unfair, then change is sought in an orderly way. Many times rules are put in place to keep you safe, to help you learn, or simply to create order. Being obedient when an authority such as your parents, teachers, or government imposes rules is your way of helping them achieve success. Trust your beliefs and obey your conscience, though, if you are told to do something that you know is wrong. (The Scout Handbook)

The Muslim is disciplined to follow Allah's commandments, the Prophet's Sunnah and those who are leading him whether it be parents, teachers, or others. It is important in Islam to respect and support leadership. This may be done through listening to our parents and teachers, helping our community leaders in projects, and following political leaders as long as they are not leading us to evil or disobeying Allah and His Messenger (s).

Allah is *Al-Malik*, The Ultimate King. He is the King of Kings and is not dependent on his subjects. He commands authority, and His creation humbly obeys Him. The Prophet (s) said, "Allah will grasp the earth and fold up the heavens with His Right Hand and proclaim, 'I Am the King. Where are the kings of the earth? Where are the tyrants? Where are the arrogant?" (Bukhari) No one will speak and the kings and rulers of this world will be left with none of their power or leadership. Thus, Allah is most worthy of our obedience.

What do Allah and the Prophet (s) say about being obedient?

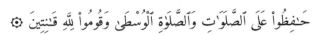

• • • • • In the Quran

حَٰفِظُواْ عَلَى ٱلصَّلَوَٰتِ وَٱلصَّلَوٰةِ ٱلْوُسْطَىٰ وَقُومُواْ لِلَّهِ قَٰنِتِينَ ۝

Take care to do your prayers, praying in the best way, and stand before Allah in devotion. (2:238)

وَأَطِيعُواْ ٱللَّهَ وَٱلرَّسُولَ لَعَلَّكُمْ تُرْحَمُونَ ۝

... And remain obedient to Allah and the Messenger, in the hope that you be shown mercy. (3:132)

مَّن يُطِعِ ٱلرَّسُولَ فَقَدْ أَطَاعَ ٱللَّهَ ۖ وَمَن تَوَلَّىٰ فَمَآ أَرْسَلْنَٰكَ عَلَيْهِمْ حَفِيظًا ۝

Whoever obeys the Messenger obeys Allah. If some pay no heed, We have not sent you to be their keeper. (4:80)

وَمَن يَقْنُتْ مِنكُنَّ لِلَّهِ وَرَسُولِهِۦ وَتَعْمَلْ صَٰلِحًا نُّؤْتِهَآ أَجْرَهَا مَرَّتَيْنِ وَأَعْتَدْنَا لَهَا رِزْقًا كَرِيمًا ۝

And whoever of you devoutly obeys Allah and His Messenger and does good, We will grant her double the reward, and We have prepared for her an honorable provision. [addressing wives of the Prophet] (33:31)

وَوَصَّيْنَا ٱلْإِنسَٰنَ بِوَٰلِدَيْهِ حَمَلَتْهُ أُمُّهُۥ وَهْنًا عَلَىٰ وَهْنٍ وَفِصَٰلُهُۥ فِى عَامَيْنِ أَنِ ٱشْكُرْ لِى وَلِوَٰلِدَيْكَ إِلَىَّ ٱلْمَصِيرُ ۞ وَإِن جَٰهَدَاكَ عَلَىٰٓ أَن تُشْرِكَ بِى مَا لَيْسَ لَكَ بِهِۦ عِلْمٌ فَلَا تُطِعْهُمَا وَصَاحِبْهُمَا فِى ٱلدُّنْيَا مَعْرُوفًا

We enjoined upon humanity to be good to his parents. His mother carried him in weakness upon weakness, and his weaning is in two years. Be grateful to Me and to your parents, for unto Me is the final destination. If they strive to make you associate with Me that for which you have no knowledge, do not obey them but still accompany them in the world with good conduct. (31:14-15)

يَٰٓأَيُّهَا ٱلَّذِينَ ءَامَنُوٓا۟ أَطِيعُوا۟ ٱللَّهَ وَأَطِيعُوا۟ ٱلرَّسُولَ وَأُو۟لِى ٱلْأَمْرِ مِنكُمْ فَإِن تَنَٰزَعْتُمْ فِى شَىْءٍ فَرُدُّوهُ إِلَى ٱللَّهِ وَٱلرَّسُولِ إِن كُنتُمْ تُؤْمِنُونَ بِٱللَّهِ وَٱلْيَوْمِ ٱلْءَاخِرِ ذَٰلِكَ خَيْرٌ وَأَحْسَنُ تَأْوِيلًا ۞

You who believe, obey Allah and the Messenger, and those in authority among you. If you are in dispute over any matter, refer it to Allah and the Messenger, if you truly believe in Allah and the Last Day: that is better and fairer in the end. (4:59)

• • • In the Hadith

1. "Whoever obeys me, has indeed obeyed Allah, and whoever disobeys me, has indeed disobeyed Allah. Whoever obeys the leader, has indeed obeyed me, and whoever disobeys the leader, has indeed disobeyed me." (Bukhari)

2. "The pleasure of the Lord is in the pleasure of the parents, and the displeasure of the Lord is in the displeasure of the parents." (Tirmithi)

3. The Prophet (s) said regarding the major sins: "They are associating partners with Allah, disobedience to parents, killing a person, and false testimony." (Bukhari)

4. "There is no obedience to anyone if it is disobedience to Allah. Verily, obedience is only in good conduct." (Bukhari)

What does it mean again?

We obey Allah's commands and follow the Prophet's Sunnah. Through Adam and Eve's experience, Allah taught us the importance of obeying Him for our own benefit. We obey Allah by following His instructions in the Quran and the example of the Prophet (s).

We respect our parents. Our parents are responsible for us and thus ask us to do many things. As a Muslim, we respect and obey our parents and follow what they ask of us.

Follow the leader. A troop or youth group cannot function nor achieve any objective without its members following the orders of its leaders. When obedience would lead us to sin or harm, we are obliged to speak up and advocate for change.

Even when making changes, we should follow rules. Muslims understand that change should come about by following the proper channels. Otherwise, disorder follows, and nothing positive can be achieved.

What's in it for me?

Having special status with Allah. In a hadith qudsi, Allah says, "My servant draws not near to Me with anything more beloved to Me than the religious duties I have enjoined upon him, and My servant continues to draw near to Me with supererogatory works so that I shall love him. When I love him, I am his hearing with which he hears, his seeing with which he sees, his hand with which he strikes and his foot with which he walks. Were he to ask of Me, I would surely give it to him, and were he to ask Me for protection, I would surely grant him it." (Bukhari)

A path to Paradise. Being dutiful and obedient to your parents can earn you a spot in Paradise. The Prophet (s) said, "May his face be rubbed in dirt! (repeated 3 times) Such is the person who has one or both his parents present in their old age, and does not enter Jannah through them [by means of serving them]." (Muslim)

Obedience to Allah gets you out of trouble. "And whosoever fears Allah and keeps his duty to Him, He will make a way for him to get out (from every difficulty). And He will provide him from (sources) he never could imagine." (65:2-3)

Life is safer and more harmonious. Imagine a life where rules are not followed, Imagine how many accidents we would have. Obedience helps promote a peaceful and safer environment for everyone.

Getting things done. When people fail to follow orders properly, it can lead to a great deal of chaos and give rise to immense frustration in any given situation and environment. By following instructions, progress is made, and big things can happen.

Let's do this

● ● ● **Salman Says**

Arrange the players in a single line formation facing the leader. Depending on the size of the groups, you may need several rows. The leader yells commands (e.g. jump, run in place, touch your toes) but the youth only respond when prefaced by "Salman says." If the leader shouts "Jump", no one should jump. However, if the leader calls out, "Salman says: Jump!", everyone should jump. Anyone making a mistake is out. As the game progresses and few players remain, the leader speeds up his commands.

Variation: Divide the group into two facing lines. One side obeys Salman, the other does not. If the leader shouts out, "Salman says: About-face!" the obeying line does an about-face, and the other line stands still. When the leader calls "About-face!" the second line does an about-face, but the first does not. The object is to see which line remains in the game longer.

● ● ● **Salman Says Advanced**

Pair up players with similar height. Distribute a balloon to each pair and have them blow it up and tie. Arrange all the pairs in a circle. Have each pair sandwich the balloon between their backs. The objective of the game is to keep the balloon between their backs without popping for the entire game. Pairs take turns to play the role of "Salman." One person from each team shouts an instruction (e.g. walk 5 steps, jog in place, do 5 squats), then the next pair and so on. Players should only respond to instructions preceded by "Salman says." Teams are eliminated if they make a mistake or the balloon drops to the ground. The winner is the last team standing. **Source: Bible Games Central**

Read more at *https://masnational.org/fn9*

• • • Blindfolds Tent

In this game, a designated person serves as the injured leader of plane crash survivors and helps guide their patrol to create shelter (i.e. to set up a simple tent). The leader cannot move, and the rest of the group is blinded by snow and smoke. Give the team plenty of time to familiarize themselves with the tent beforehand. Then run a timed attempt, the starting point being the tent in the bag. Only blindfolded youth can touch the tent, and the leader should be seated and only give instructions. The leader must guide his or her team to construct the tent in under 15 minutes. You can have each group compete to see who can assemble their tent the fastest. (*Supplies: tent(s), blindfolds*) **Source: Biz Fluent**

Read more at *https://masnational.org/23r*

• • • Capture the Flag

To host a round of the classic game of capture the flag, you need a field or wooded area. Read up on the basic outline and variations of this popular team game. Elaborate games of capture the flag may last several hours. Adding scouts, two-way radios, paintball guns or water pistols will add excitement and novelty to the game. Game facilitators or referees can look for learning opportunities to discuss teamwork and the importance of leadership and obedience. Upon completing the game, relate the story of the archers at the Battle of Uhud and how the archers not following orders cost the Muslims their victory. Look for situations in the game that resemble the archers in Uhud and other scenarios related to obedience.

? Let's reflect

1. What are some areas where you find it easy to obey Allah? What areas are more difficult?

2. Sometimes it is easy to obey parents, teachers, leaders, and other times it is more difficult. What makes obedience challenging? What types of commands do you tend to question? What things do you hesitate to obey? What areas of disobedience do you often make excuses for? What makes it easier to be obedient?

3. How do you make things right after having disobeyed a leader or a parent?

4. Share a story about a time when you found it hard to be obedient to Allah or your parents.

5. Without sharing any names, describe how a youth might be disobedient. How would a disobedient youth affect the patrol or group? The troop?

6. Does disagreeing with the leader mean you are disobedient? Why/why not? When do youth who share a different opinion become disobedient?

7. Think of something you are finding hard to be obedient with (e.g. swearing, stealing). Write down one thing you can do this week to build up your obedience muscles.

8. How is Allah the King of All Kings? What names and attributes of Allah remind us of His Kingship and dominion? Discuss how *Allah is Al-Malik* (The King) and *Malik-ul-Mulk* (The King of Kings) and how we can channel those names of Allah in our daily lives.

 Let's make dua

1. O Allah! Director of the hearts, direct our hearts to your obedience. (Muslim)

اللّٰهُمَّ مُصَرِّفَ القُلُوبِ صَرِّفْ قُلُوبَنَا عَلَى طَاعَتِكَ

2. O Allah, apportion to us enough reverence as should serve as a barrier between us and acts of disobedience; and apportion to us enough obedience as will take us to Your Jannah, and such conviction as will make it easy for us to bear the calamities of this world. O Allah! Let us enjoy our hearing, our sight and our strength as long as You keep us alive and leave them to inherit us. Let retaliation fall upon those who oppress us and support us against those who are hostile toward us. Let no calamity afflict our faith. Let not the world be our main concern nor the extent of

our knowledge. And do not allow those who are unmerciful toward us to rule over us. (Tirmithi)

اللَّهُمَّ اقْسِمْ لَنَا مِنْ خَشْيَتِكَ مَا تَحُولُ بِهِ بَيْنَنَا وَبَيْنَ مَعَاصِيكَ، وَمِنْ طَاعَتِكَ مَا تُبَلِّغُنَا بِهِ جَنَّتَكَ، وَمِنَ الْيَقِينِ مَا تُهَوِّنُ بِهِ عَلَيْنَا مَصَائِبَ الدُّنْيَا، اللَّهُمَّ مَتِّعْنَا بِأَسْمَاعِنَا، وَأَبْصَارِنَا، وَقُوَّاتِنَا مَا أَحْيَيْتَنَا، وَاجْعَلْهُ الْوَارِثَ مِنَّا، وَاجْعَلْ ثَأْرَنَا عَلَى مَنْ ظَلَمَنَا، وَانْصُرْنَا عَلَى مَنْ عَادَانَا، وَلَا تَجْعَلْ مُصِيبَتَنَا فِي دِينِنَا، وَلَا تَجْعَلِ الدُّنْيَا أَكْبَرَ هَمِّنَا، وَلَا مَبْلَغَ عِلْمِنَا، وَلَا تُسَلِّطْ عَلَيْنَا مَنْ لَا يَرْحَمُنَا.

3. My Lord, have mercy upon them (parents) as they brought me up when I was small. (17:24)

رَبِّ ارْحَمْهُمَا كَمَا رَبَّيَانِي صَغِيرًا

4. The Prophet (s) used to say immediately following the witr prayer: *Subhaan al-Malik al-Quddoos* (Glory is to the King, the Holy) three times, and raising and extending his voice on the third time and then saying: *Rabb al-malaa'ikati warrooh* (Lord of the angels and the Spirit [Gabriel]). (An-Nasaa'i)

سبحانَ الملكُ القدوسُ رَبُّ الملائكةِ والروح

Let's teach it

A Scout is Obedient
Suggested Curriculum

The content included for each characteristic can span several scouting seasons. In this section, we have included a suggested curriculum for an entire month to simplify your planning. On week 4, we assumed the troop or youth group would participate in a campout or outdoor activity. The next section is a blank curriculum for you to design your own.

Week 1: Introduction to Obedience

Open with Quran	4:59
Youth Talk	Hadith #1
Leader Talk	• Scout Law definition and Islamic perspective • What does it mean again? • What's in it for me?
Closing Dua	Dua #3

Week 2: Obedience to Parents

Open with Quran	31:14-15
Youth Talk	Hadith #2, 3
Leader Talk	Racing to Obey
Activity	Salman Says Advanced
Closing Dua	Dua #3

Week 3: Obedience to Leaders

Open with Quran	4:59
Youth Talk	Hadith #4
Activity	Let's Reflect #7
Closing Dua	Dua #3

Week 4 Camp: Bringing it All Together

Open with Quran	3:132
Youth Talk	• What's in it for me? • Let's Reflect #9
Leader Talk	The Archers at Uhud
Activity	Capture the Flag
Closing Dua	Dua #3 (After each prayer)
Campfire	Let's Reflect #2

Let's teach it

A Scout is Obedient

Design your own Curriculum

Week 1:

Open with Quran	
Youth Talk	
Leader Talk	
Activity	
Closing Dua	

Week 2:

Open with Quran	
Youth Talk	
Leader Talk	
Activity	
Closing Dua	

Week 3:

Open with Quran	
Youth Talk	
Leader Talk	
Activity	
Closing Dua	

Week 4 Camp:

Open with Quran	
Youth Talk	
Leader Talk	
Activity	
Closing Dua	
Campfire	

A Scout is Cheerful

A Scout is cheerful. A Scout looks for the bright side of life. A Scout cheerfully does assigned tasks and tries to make others happy, too. You know you cannot always have your way, but a cheerful attitude can make the time seem to pass more quickly and can even turn a task you dislike into a lot of fun. You have a choice whether to enjoy life's experiences and challenges. It is always easier and much more enjoyable to decide from the start to be cheerful whenever you can. (The Scout Handbook)

The Muslim has a positive perspective on life and is a joy to be around even during challenging times. Islam teaches us that even smiling at people is a good act and will be rewarded. Having such an attitude and demeanor when working or serving others is contagious and brings about a pleasant atmosphere.

Allah is *Al-Muhyee*, the Giver of life, and we should do our best to cherish that life. Allah is *Ash-Shakoor*, The Most Appreciative, and one way that we show our appreciation of others is through cheerfulness and making them happy.

What do Allah and the Prophet (s) say about being cheerful?

• • • • In the Quran

وَءَاتَىٰكُم مِّن كُلِّ مَا سَأَلْتُمُوهُ ۚ وَإِن تَعُدُّواْ نِعْمَتَ ٱللَّهِ لَا تُحْصُوهَآ ۗ إِنَّ ٱلْإِنسَٰنَ لَظَلُومٌ كَفَّارٌ ۞

...And if you should count the favor of Allah, you could not enumerate them. Indeed, mankind is [generally] most unjust and ungrateful. (14:34)

قُل بِفَضْلِ ٱللَّهِ وَبِرَحْمَتِهِۦ فَبِذَٰلِكَ فَلْيَفْرَحُواْ هُوَ خَيْرٌ مِّمَّا يَجْمَعُونَ ۞

Say, "In Allah's grace and mercy let them rejoice. That is far better than whatever wealth they amass."(10:58)

قَوْلٌ مَّعْرُوفٌ وَمَغْفِرَةٌ خَيْرٌ مِّن صَدَقَةٍ يَتْبَعُهَآ أَذًى ۗ وَٱللَّهُ غَنِيٌّ حَلِيمٌ ۞

Kind words and forgiveness are better than charity followed by injury. And Allah is Self-Sufficient, Most Forbearing. (2:263)

كُتِبَ عَلَيْكُمُ ٱلْقِتَالُ وَهُوَ كُرْهٌ لَّكُمْ ۖ وَعَسَىٰٓ أَن تَكْرَهُواْ شَيْـًٔا وَهُوَ خَيْرٌ لَّكُمْ ۖ وَعَسَىٰٓ أَن تُحِبُّواْ شَيْـًٔا وَهُوَ شَرٌّ لَّكُمْ ۗ وَٱللَّهُ يَعْلَمُ وَأَنتُمْ لَا تَعْلَمُونَ ۞

Fighting has been made obligatory upon you [believers], though you dislike it. Perhaps you dislike something which is good for you and like something which is bad for you. Allah knows and you do not know. (2:216)

1. "Verily, you cannot enrich all of the people with your wealth, but rather you enrich them with your cheerful faces and good character." (al-Bayhaqi)

2. "Do not consider any act of piety insignificant, even if it is meeting your brother with a cheerful countenance." (Muslim)

3. "Every good deed is a charitable donation. It is a good deed to meet your brother with a smiling face and pour from your pail into your brother's pail." (Tirmithi)

4. Abdullah ibn al-Harith ibn Jaz' said about the Prophet (s), "I never met anyone who smiled more than the Messenger of Allah, peace and blessings be upon him." (Tirmithi)

5. "Amazing is the affair of the believer! Verily all of his life is good, and this applies to no one except the believer. If something good befalls him he is grateful and that is good for him. If something harmful befalls him he is patient and that is good for him." (Muslim)

6. "Verily, thinking well about Allah is part of the excellent worship of Allah." (Tirmithi)

7. "Allah Almighty says: I am as My servant expects of Me. If he thinks good of Me, he will have it. If he thinks evil of Me, he will have it." (Ibn Hibban)

8. It was said about the Prophet's Companions: They used to joke around by throwing melon rinds at each other. But when things got serious, they would be men. (Sahih Adab al-Mufrad)

What does it mean again?

Cheerfulness allows you to see opportunity during difficulty. Nothing happens without the will of Allah. This mindset enables a Muslim to navigate challenges with optimism and reliance on Allah.

Less fussing. This is the essence of cheerful service in which a Muslim strives to perform a deed knowing Allah is watching and thus avoids complaining.

Ain't no grouch! A Muslim has an uplifting personality so that others enjoy their company during good and bad times. One way to uplift others is by being lighthearted or playful.

Tell Me A Story

• • • A Stubborn Boulder

During a stressful moment, the Prophet (s) lifted the spirits of his Companions. (pg. 234)

• • • A Boy and his Sparrow

A little boy loses his pet sparrow and is cheered up by the Prophet (s). (pg. 235)

What's in it for me?

Admiration of others. The Prophet (s) said: "You will never attain the attraction of people through your wealth, but rather through your cheerful countenance." (al-Hakim)

Less stress. Cortisol, the stress hormone, decreases in response to laughter and smiling.

Happier Mood = Healthier Life. A happier mood leads to lower blood pressure and a stronger immune system.

Makes difficult tasks easier and more pleasant. It goes without saying: having fun while doing a difficult task makes it easier to get through.

Let's do this

• • • Moratorium on Complaining

Challenge your youth to spend the entire camp without complaining. Have youth document when they complain and debrief the experience at the end of camp realizing how much we complain versus being grateful.

• • • Gratitude Attitude

Give each person a pen and piece of paper and ask them to title it: "What I'm Thankful For" with 3 column headers: People, Things, and Other. Under "People," list names of family, mentors, friends, coaches, teachers and role models you're thankful for. Under "Things," list things such as your house, A/C, food, clothes, your body, etc. Under "Other," write things like freedom, faith, etc. Now, for the next few days, challenge the youth to carry this list with them and reflect on it daily—morning, lunch, and at bedtime. At the next meeting, discuss if anyone noticed any changes in attitude. (*Supplies: paper, pens*)

Source: Character Education Lessons

Read more at *https://masnational.org/0mu*

• • • Macho Man Contest

In this hilarious activity, youth test their resolve in holding a straight face while eating a lemon. Select four volunteers and give each half of a lemon. While facing the audience, they peel the lemon and eat it with the least amount of facial expressions. The audience votes for the winner. Award each of them a cracker to remove the sour taste. During the debrief, ask: How do people react when you hurt them with your words or actions? (Some get angry but get over it. Some hold their anger inside. Some try to work things out. Some deal with it and then put it behind them.) What's the healthiest way to deal with hurt feelings? When life serves you lemons, you can either be miserable inside or make lemonade. Choose to make lemonade and you will be the happiest. (*Supplies: lemons, crackers*)

Let's reflect

1. How can you be cheerful when doing something you don't want to do?

2. When is it difficult to be cheerful? Can you be cheerful during the most difficult of times? Explain.

3. Who is someone you know who is cheerful? How does that person make you feel?

4. What is the difference between being cheerful and happy?

5. Are the jokers in the group the only cheerful ones? Can others who are more serious be cheerful?

6. What can you do on a regular basis to maintain a cheerful attitude? What are practical steps we can take at camp?

7. One of Allah's attributes is *Ash-Shakur* (The Most Appreciative); how does that relate to being cheerful? One of Allah's attributes is *Al-Ghafoor* (The Great Forgiver); how can you live by that name and how does it affect your attitude? When we know Allah as *Al-Muhyee* (The Giver of Life), how can we honor that name in our interactions and how can it shape our behavior? How can we channel these names of Allah in our daily lives?

Let's make dua

1. "O Allah! Indeed I am Your servant Son of Your male servant and female servant. My forelock is in Your Hand (i.e. You have control over me) and Your Judgment upon me is assured, and Your Decree upon me is just. I ask You with every name that You have named Yourself with, or revealed in Your Book (Quran), or taught to any of Your creation, or kept with Yourself in the knowledge of the unseen that is with You that you make the Quran the life of my heart, and the light of my chest, and the banisher of my sadness, and the reliever of my distress."

اللّٰهُمَّ إِنِّي عَبْدُكَ، ابْنُ عَبْدِكَ، ابْنُ أَمَتِكَ، نَاصِيَتِي بِيَدِكَ، مَاضٍ فِيَّ حُكْمُكَ، عَدْلٌ فِيَّ قَضَاؤُكَ، أَسْأَلُكَ بِكُلِّ اسْمٍ هُوَ لَكَ سَمَّيْتَ بِهِ نَفْسَكَ، أَوْ أَنْزَلْتَهُ فِي كِتَابِكَ، أَوْ عَلَّمْتَهُ أَحَدًا مِنْ خَلْقِكَ، أَوِ اسْتَأْثَرْتَ بِهِ فِي عِلْمِ الْغَيْبِ عِنْدَكَ، أَنْ تَجْعَلَ الْقُرْآنَ رَبِيعَ قَلْبِي، وَنُورَ صَدْرِي، وَجَلَاءَ حُزْنِي، وَذَهَابَ هَمِّي

2. I am pleased with Allah as [my] Lord, with Islam as [my] Religion and Muhammad (s) as Prophet and Messenger. According to a hadith, whosoever recites the above thrice in the morning and evening, it is upon Allah to please him on the Day of Judgment, and admission into Jannah is a certainty for him. (Ahmad)

رَضِيتُ بِاللهِ رَبًّا، وَبِالْإِسْلَامِ دِينًا، وَبِمُحَمَّدٍ صلى الله عليه وسلم نَبِيًّا

3. Lord, inspire me to be thankful for the blessings You have granted me and my parents, and to do good deeds that please You; admit me by Your grace into the ranks of Your righteous servants. (27:19)

وَقَالَ رَبِّ أَوْزِعْنِيٓ أَنْ أَشْكُرَ نِعْمَتَكَ ٱلَّتِيٓ أَنْعَمْتَ عَلَيَّ وَعَلَىٰ وَٰلِدَيَّ وَأَنْ أَعْمَلَ صَٰلِحًا تَرْضَىٰهُ وَأَدْخِلْنِى بِرَحْمَتِكَ فِى عِبَادِكَ ٱلصَّٰلِحِينَ

Let's teach it

A Scout is Cheerful

Suggested Curriculum

The content included for each characteristic can span several scouting seasons. In this section, we have included a suggested curriculum for an entire month to simplify your planning. On week 4, we assumed the troop or youth group would participate in a campout or outdoor activity. The next section is a blank curriculum for you to design your own.

Week 1: Introduction to Cheerful

Open with Quran	14:34 10:58
Youth Talk	Hadith #5
Leader Talk	• Scout Law definition and Islamic perspective • What does it mean again? • What's in it for me?
Activity	Let's Reflect #4
Closing Dua	Dua #2

Week 2: Cheerful and Positivity

Open with Quran	2:216
Youth Talk	Hadith #6, 7
Activity	Gratitude Attitude
Closing Dua	Dua #2

Week 3: Cheerful Service

Open with Quran	2:263
Youth Talk	Hadith #8
Leader Talk	Stubborn Boulder
Activity	Let's Reflect #1
Closing Dua	Dua #2

Week 4 Camp: Bringing it All Together

Open with Quran	14:34 10:58
Youth Talk	• What's in it for me? • Let's Reflect #7
Leader Talk	A Boy and his Sparrow
Activity	Macho Man Contest
Closing Dua	Dua #2 (After each prayer)
Campfire	Let's Reflect #3

Let's teach it

A Scout is Cheerful

Design your own Curriculum

Week 1:

Open with Quran	
Youth Talk	
Leader Talk	
Activity	
Closing Dua	

Week 2:

Open with Quran	
Youth Talk	
Leader Talk	
Activity	
Closing Dua	

Week 3:

Open with Quran	
Youth Talk	
Leader Talk	
Activity	
Closing Dua	

Week 4 Camp:

Open with Quran	
Youth Talk	
Leader Talk	
Activity	
Closing Dua	
Campfire	

A Scout is Thrifty

A Scout is thrifty. Scouts work to pay their own way and to help others. Scouts save for the future. A Scout protects and conserves natural resources and is careful in the use of time, money, and property. Paying your own way with money you have earned gives you independence and pride. Even if you have only a few dollars, you have enough to save a bit for the future and even to share a bit with others—although what you share doesn't have to be in cash. Volunteering your time and talent can be just as valuable as donating money. (The Scout Handbook)

In Islam, being thrifty is connected with being thankful to Allah for His blessings and being always conscious that our blessings are not for us to squander and enjoy alone, but to share with others and to build a better future. We will be questioned about every single dollar we spend, every minute of our time, and every bite of food we eat or throw away.

Allah is *Al-Ghani* (The Self-Sufficient) and *Al-Hakeem* (The Wise). He is in need of no one, and we are completely dependent upon Him for our sustenance. Allah carries out His divine will in the best way, at the right time and place.

What do Allah and the Prophet (s) say about being thrifty?

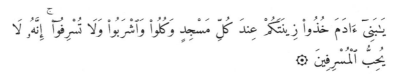

• • • • • In the Quran

يَـٰبَنِىٓ ءَادَمَ خُذُواْ زِينَتَكُمْ عِندَ كُلِّ مَسْجِدٍ وَكُلُواْ وَٱشْرَبُواْ وَلَا تُسْرِفُوٓاْ إِنَّهُۥ لَا يُحِبُّ ٱلْمُسْرِفِينَ ۞

O Children of Adam! Dress properly whenever you are at worship. Eat and drink, but do not waste. Surely, He does not like the wasteful. (7:31)

وَٱلَّذِينَ إِذَآ أَنفَقُواْ لَمْ يُسْرِفُواْ وَلَمْ يَقْتُرُواْ وَكَانَ بَيْنَ ذَٰلِكَ قَوَامًا ۞

They are those who spend neither wastefully nor stingily, but moderately in between. (25:67)

ثُمَّ لَتُسْـَٔلُنَّ يَوْمَئِذٍ عَنِ ٱلنَّعِيمِ ۞

Then, on that Day, you will definitely be questioned about your worldly pleasures. (102:8)

إِنَّ ٱلْمُبَذِّرِينَ كَانُوٓاْ إِخْوَٰنَ ٱلشَّيَـٰطِينِ ۖ وَكَانَ ٱلشَّيْطَـٰنُ لِرَبِّهِۦ كَفُورًا ۞

Surely, the wasteful are brothers to the devils. And the Devil is ever ungrateful to his Lord. (17:27)

هَٰٓأَنتُمْ هَٰٓؤُلَآءِ تُدْعَوْنَ لِتُنفِقُوا۟ فِى سَبِيلِ ٱللَّهِ فَمِنكُم مَّن يَبْخَلُ ۖ وَمَن يَبْخَلْ فَإِنَّمَا يَبْخَلُ عَن نَّفْسِهِۦ ۚ وَٱللَّهُ ٱلْغَنِىُّ وَأَنتُمُ ٱلْفُقَرَآءُ ۚ وَإِن تَتَوَلَّوْا۟ يَسْتَبْدِلْ قَوْمًا غَيْرَكُمْ ثُمَّ لَا يَكُونُوٓا۟ أَمْثَٰلَكُم ۞

Here you are, being invited to donate in the cause of Allah. Still some of you withhold. And whoever does so, it is only to their own loss. For Allah is the Self-Sufficient, whereas you stand in need of Him. If you still turn away, He will replace you with another people. And they will not be like you. (47:38)

وَٱلْعَصْرِ ۞ إِنَّ ٱلْإِنسَٰنَ لَفِى خُسْرٍ ۞ إِلَّا ٱلَّذِينَ ءَامَنُوا۟ وَعَمِلُوا۟ ٱلصَّٰلِحَٰتِ وَتَوَاصَوْا۟ بِٱلْحَقِّ وَتَوَاصَوْا۟ بِٱلصَّبْرِ ۞

By the declining day, man is [deep] in loss, except for those who believe, do good deeds, urge one another to the truth, and urge one another to steadfastness. (103:1-3)

• • • In the Hadith

1. "The son of Adam does not fill any vessel worse than his stomach. It is sufficient for the son of Adam to eat a few mouthfuls to keep him going. If he must (fill his stomach), then let him fill one third with food, one third with drink and one third with air." (Tirmithi)

2. The Messenger (s) passed by Sa'd while he was performing ablution and said, "What is this excess?" Sa'd responded, "Is there excess in water for

ablution?" The Prophet said, "Yes, even if you were on the banks of a flowing river." (Ibn Majah)

3. "It is far better for you to take your rope, go to the mountains, carry firewood on your back, sell it and thereby save your face from shame, than beg from people, regardless of whether they give to you or refuse you. The upper hand is better than the lower one. Begin charity with those who are under your care.' It was asked: 'Who are those that are under my care?' He (s) replied: 'Your wife and those under your guardianship." (Muslim)

4. "Eating food with people brings about abundance. One person's food portion is enough for two people, and two people's food portion is enough for four." (Agreed upon)

5. "Take advantage of five before five: your youth before your old age, your health before your sickness, your wealth before your poverty, your free time before your busyness, and your life before your death." (al-Albani)

What does it mean again?

A Muslim doesn't overspend. We need to think twice before we buy anything. Reuse, recycle, borrow, and when we spend, try to find the best prices.

The more you spend, the greedier you get. Wasting leads to greed, greed leads to non-contentment, and non-contentment leads to more spending and wasting.

It takes discipline and good planning to be thrifty. A Muslim is self-reliant and disciplines his *nafs* (self and desires). He plans well so that he has enough for future obligations and charity.

Thrifty doesn't mean stingy. Thrifty doesn't mean that you never spend anything and only buy cheap things.

Thrifty is being generous. Being thrifty includes thanking Allah for His blessings by sharing them with others and making sure to budget the right amount for *zakah* and charity.

Thrifty is respecting resources. This entire world is a trust. We must exercise moderation in everything we consume: water, the types of food we eat, our clothing, and so on. In addition to being moderate, we must not be wasteful.

Thrifty is being careful with time. Our time is limited and every minute counts. A Muslim is worried about their time and makes sure to use it wisely.

Tell Me A Story

What's in it for me?

Allah is going to be pleased with us. You are
showing Allah that you are grateful for the blessings
He has bestowed on you.

Less stress and fewer financial worries. By living
below your means, you can save money on the
side to handle challenging financial situations. Not
caring too much about wealth is good for your mind
and soul.

Good for the environment. Recycling, reusing,
carpooling and buying fewer things all reduce air
and water pollution.

Benefit to humanity. The less fortunate can benefit
from your generosity whether it be a monetary
contribution or just donating and sharing your
belongings.

Let's do this

• • • **Stop W³!**
(Wasting Water in *Wudu*)

Have each youth make *wudu* and estimate how much
water they are using. Then show them an efficient way
to make *wudu* by turning the tap on low, stopping the
tap when not using, using a bowl, etc. Then have the
youth make *wudu* again, comparing how much water
they are saving.

• • • **I earned it!**

Instead of asking your parents, save up money to pay
for your next summer camp yourself. For example, work
with your fellow scouts to earn money by providing a
service to the community.

• • • **Paying it forward**

Organize a fundraiser to help a local nonprofit or the
needy in your community.

• • • **Camp Smarter**

Brainstorm how the next meeting or camp can be more
thrifty: bring your own water bottles, make sure food
is not wasted, try fixing any camping equipment before
buying a new one.

• • • Buy Less Stuff

Watch this 15-minute reporting about the garbage crisis by searching "Is Recycling Worth it Anymore" on npr.org. How do you feel after watching the video? What can we do to help? Another impactful video is True Cost, a 50-minute documentary on the clothing industry.

• • • Reuse Workshop

Before meeting, ask every youth to bring an old, clean pair of pants that they don't wear anymore, without saying what the clothing will be used for. Have a table with scissors, needles and thread, fabric glue, and invite youth to figure out how to repurpose the clothing and reuse or pass on to someone else.

• • • Share with Three

At meal or snack time, without explaining the activity, invite a third of the troop or youth group to go get their food. Then, instead of allowing the others to get food, tell the youth group or troop that is all the food they will get and they will have to share what they have. Discuss afterward whether the food was enough, what the difficulties were and what surprised them.

Let's reflect

1. List some synonyms for the word thrifty. Many of the synonyms provided will be negative in connotation. Why is that?

2. The word "thrift" comes from the word "thrive," to live and grow and flourish. How does the scout definition support this?

3. Think about all of your belongings. Do they fall into the category of a want or a need? Can you do with less? How can you demonstrate being thrifty?

4. On a scale of 1 to 10, how much do you struggle with being thrifty? Explain.

5. Explain how certain merit badges teach you about being thrifty.

6. Talk about the last time you got Eid or birthday money. How did you spend it? Allow everyone to share. How would you spend it differently after learning what it means to be thrifty?

7. What names and attributes of Allah remind us of the importance of being thrifty and conscious of our consumption? Discuss how Allah is *Al-Ghani* (The Enricher), *Al-Mani`* (The Withholder), *Ar-Razzaq* (The Provider), *Al-Hakeem* (The Wise), *Al-Wakeel* (The Trustee) and how we can channel those names of Allah in our daily lives.

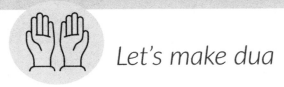

Let's make dua

1. O Allah, we seek refuge in You from anxiety, sorrow, weakness, laziness, miserliness, cowardice, and the burden of debts and from being overpowered by men. (Bukhari and others)

اللّٰهُمَّ إِنَّا نَعُوذُ بِكَ مِنَ الهَمِّ وَالحَزَنِ وَالجُبْنِ وَالبُخْلِ، وَنَعُوذُ بِكَ مِن غَلَبَةِ الدَّيْنِ وَقَهرِ الرِّجَالِ

2. Provide for us sustenance, for You are the best of sustainers. (5:114)

وَارْزُقْنَا وَأَنْتَ خَيْرُ الرَّازِقِينَ

3. O Allah, make what is halal enough for me, keep me away from haram, and make me independent of everyone except for You. (Tirmithi)

اللهم اكْفِنِي بِحَلَالِكَ عن حَرَامِكَ ، وَأَغْنِنِي بِفَضْلِكَ عَمَّنْ سِوَاكَ

4. O Allah! I ask You for knowledge that is of benefit, good provision and deeds that will be accepted. (Ibn Majah)

اللّهُمَّ إِنِّي أَسْأَلُكَ عِلْماً نَافِعاً، وَرِزْقاً طَيِّباً، وَعَمَلاً مُتَقَبَّلا

5. All praise is due to Allah, who was the One who satisfied us, blessed us, and was generous to us.

الْحَمْدُ لِلَّهِ الَّذِي هُوَ أَشْبَعَنَا وَأَرْوَانَا وَأَنْعَمَ عَلَيْنَا وَأَفْضَلَ

Let's teach it

A Scout is Thrifty
Suggested Curriculum

The content included for each characteristic can span several scouting seasons. In this section, we have included a suggested curriculum for an entire month to simplify your planning. On week 4, we assumed the troop or youth group would participate in a campout or outdoor activity. The next section is a blank curriculum for you to design your own.

Week 1: Introduction to Thrifty

Open with Quran	7:31, 25:67, 17:27
Youth Talk	Hadith #1, 2
Leader Talk	• Scout Law definition and Islamic perspective • What does it mean again? • What's in it for me?
Closing Dua	Dua #1

Week 2: Not Being Wasteful

Open with Quran	7:31, 25:67, 17:27
Youth Talk	Hadith #4
Activity	Incredible Management
Closing Dua	Dua #1

Week 3: Being Self-reliant

Open with Quran	13:11, 47:38
Youth Talk	Hadith #3
Closing Dua	Dua #1

Week 4 Camp: Bringing it All Together

Open with Quran	7:31, 25:67, 13:11
Youth Talk	Hadith #5
Leader Talk	A Delicious Meal at Abu Ayoob's
Activity	• Stop W^3! • Camp Smarter
Closing Dua	Dua #1 (After each prayer)
Campfire	• Let's Reflect #3 • Let's Reflect #7

Let's teach it

A Scout is Thrifty

Design your own Curriculum

Week 1:	
Open with Quran	
Youth Talk	
Leader Talk	
Activity	
Closing Dua	

Week 2:	
Open with Quran	
Youth Talk	
Leader Talk	
Activity	
Closing Dua	

Week 3:

Open with Quran	
Youth Talk	
Leader Talk	
Activity	
Closing Dua	

Week 4 Camp:

Open with Quran	
Youth Talk	
Leader Talk	
Activity	
Closing Dua	
Campfire	

A Scout is Brave

A Scout is brave. A Scout faces danger even when afraid. A Scout does the right thing even when doing the wrong thing or doing nothing would be easier. Bravery doesn't have to mean saving someone's life at risk to your own. While that is definitely brave, you are also being brave when you speak up to stop someone from being bullied or when you do what is right in spite of what others say. You are brave when you speak the truth and when you admit a mistake and apologize for it. And you show true courage when you defend the rights of others. (The Scout Handbook)

For a Muslim, bravery stems from seeking the pleasure of Allah and fearing none but Him. As Muslims, we recognize being uncomfortable when encountering a difficult situation, but it's the reliance on Allah that helps us overcome our obstacles. Courage and bravery go hand in hand with steadfastness and perseverance.

Allah is *Al-Qawiyy* (The Strong) and *Al-Azeez* (The All-Mighty and Honorable). These two names of strength and honor are often paired together. Real strength is not suited except to those who are honorable; *Al-Qawiyy* uses His Strength in the most honorable ways to show His perfect might. When we need courage, we can derive the most honorable strength from *Al-Qawiyy*. Lastly, Allah is *Al-Mateen* (The Firm) which reminds us that when we feel weak, we can hold on to Him to stay firm and steadfast.

What do Allah and the Prophet (s) say about being brave?

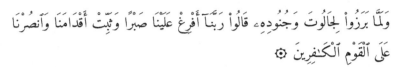

• • • • • In the Quran

وَلَمَّا بَرَزُواْ لِجَالُوتَ وَجُنُودِهِۦ قَالُواْ رَبَّنَآ أَفْرِغْ عَلَيْنَا صَبْرًا وَثَبِّتْ أَقْدَامَنَا وَٱنصُرْنَا عَلَى ٱلْقَوْمِ ٱلْكَـٰفِرِينَ ۞

And when they met Goliath and his warriors, they said, 'Our Lord, pour patience on us, make us stand firm, and help us against the disbelievers.' (2:250)

يَـٰبُنَىَّ أَقِمِ ٱلصَّلَوٰةَ وَأْمُرْ بِٱلْمَعْرُوفِ وَٱنْهَ عَنِ ٱلْمُنكَرِ وَٱصْبِرْ عَلَىٰ مَآ أَصَابَكَ إِنَّ ذَٰلِكَ مِنْ عَزْمِ ٱلْأُمُورِ ۞

O my child, establish the prayer and command to what is fair and forbid what is deplorable, and be patient over what has befallen you; indeed, that is of the matters requiring determination. (31:17)

يَـٰٓأَيُّهَا ٱلَّذِينَ ءَامَنُواْ ٱصْبِرُواْ وَصَابِرُواْ وَرَابِطُواْ وَٱتَّقُواْ ٱللَّهَ لَعَلَّكُمْ تُفْلِحُونَ ۞

O believers! Patiently endure, persevere, stand on guard, and be mindful of Allah, so you may be successful. (3:200)

فَلَا تَخْشَوُاْ ٱلنَّاسَ وَٱخْشَوْنِ وَلَا تَشْتَرُواْ بِـَٔايَـٰتِى ثَمَنًا قَلِيلًا

... So do not fear the people; fear Me! Nor trade my revelations for a fleeting gain... (5:44)

وَلَنَبْلُوَنَّكُم بِشَىْءٍ مِّنَ ٱلْخَوْفِ وَٱلْجُوعِ وَنَقْصٍ مِّنَ ٱلْأَمْوَٰلِ وَٱلْأَنفُسِ وَٱلثَّمَرَٰتِ وَبَشِّرِ ٱلصَّٰبِرِينَ ۞ ٱلَّذِينَ إِذَآ أَصَٰبَتْهُم مُّصِيبَةٌ قَالُوٓا۟ إِنَّا لِلَّهِ وَإِنَّآ إِلَيْهِ رَٰجِعُونَ ۞

"And We will surely test you with something of fear and hunger and a loss of wealth and lives and fruits, but give good tidings to the patient...Who, when disaster strikes them, say, 'Indeed we belong to Allah, and indeed to Him we will return." (2:155-156)

In the Hadith

1. "The strong believer is better and more loved by Allah, the Almighty, than the weak one, and there is good in both. Keenly pursue what benefits you, seek Help from Allah, and do not lose hope. If something befalls you, do not say "if only I had done such and such," for "if only" opens the door to the shaitan." (Muslim) (note that this hadith is not referring to physical strength alone but to determination and perseverance)

2. "Let not fear of the people prevent one of you from saying the truth, if he knows it." (Ahmad)

3. The Prophet (s) comforted Abu Bakr in the cave while the disbelievers were surrounding it, by saying courageously to him while being confident of the protection of Allah, the Almighty: "Do not grieve; indeed Allah is with us."

What does it mean again?

Face difficult situations even when you feel afraid. Do what you think is right despite what others might be doing or saying.

Man up! Woman up! The Muslim musters up the courage to face his or her fear while relying on Allah.

Peer pressure...what peer pressure? A Muslim does not succumb to negative peer pressure, instead seeking to do what is honorable.

Admit mistakes and be honest about it! True courage is when you make a blunder and you 'fess up.

FEAR has two possible meanings:
1) Forget Everything And Run
      and
2) Face Everything And Rise.

The Muslim chooses to live by the second one.

Tell Me A Story

Help from Allah. Doing the right thing earns you Allah's pleasure and assistance during challenging situations.

Personal growth. By tackling your fears, you expand your comfort zone and thus grow.

Sound heart. You become at peace with yourself and have a clear conscience because you are not afraid to speak the truth.

Live life on your own terms. You are not worried about what others think and thus you are more content.

Get things done! You become a person of action, not afraid of taking a risk, trying something new and learning in the process. Be courageous to learn from your failures. Know that failing fast means learning and gets you one step closer to your goal.

Let's do this

• • • The Courageous Egg

In this activity, teach your youth that it takes courage to do the right thing. A courageous person will stand out from the rest and rise to the top. Place an unboiled egg in the middle of a glass jar completely covered by uncooked rice. Explain that the egg represents someone who is hanging with bad company. One day the group starts bullying others, and the egg is displeased so he tells them to stop (cup your hands and tap the sides of the jar; the egg will rise up from the rice with each tap). Next, the group of friends starts cheating and telling lies. Each time, the egg refuses to go along with his friends and stands up for what's right (tap each time so the egg rises). Continue until the egg has completely risen above the rice. Debrief by asking youth to share examples of when they had to be brave. How did they get through it? What stops you from being brave? (*Supplies: Wide mouthed glass or jar, uncooked rice, egg.*)

Source: Markkula Center for Applied Ethics

Read more at *https://masnational.org/f2v*

• • • On a roll

Show the youth a piece of paper and ask them if there is any way the paper can hold up the book, using only one hand to hold the paper. You can ask for several volunteers to try; soon they will realize there is no way. Now take the paper and roll it tightly into a tube with a diameter of about 1 to 1/2 inches. Hold the tube in one hand and carefully place the book on top of the open end of the tube. It should support the book. Relate this to the ability we all have to manage our weaknesses and show courage. The paper at first is flimsy and easy to crush and overwhelm. But, just as the paper can be rolled into a sturdy tube, we can work to add muscle to our weaknesses, developing a stronger backbone that holds up to pressure. Debrief by asking: What did you think at first when the activity was explained? How can we leverage our strengths to overcome our weaknesses? Do you have more courage than you think? (*Supplies: One sheet of copy paper, small book*)

Source: Character Council

Read more at *https://masnational.org/qi2*

• • • Expand your comfort zone

Try something new today that takes you out of your comfort zone. (e.g. try a new food, a merit badge that makes you uncomfortable, learn a new skill and share with your troop, give a speech, raise money for a worthwhile organization)

• • • Where does it fall on the Courage-meter?

Have each youth rank the following from most courageous (1) to least courageous (8) and have them discuss their reasoning.

- Volunteering to call the *athaan*
- Approaching a potential new friend and introducing yourself

- Saying no to vaping when all your friends are doing it
- Trying to skateboard in front of your friends when you have never tried it before
- Admitting to your parents or teachers that you told a lie
- Helping someone who is being bullied
- Being the only student in your class who wears hijab
- Stepping aside to pray at a sporting event

• • • Crush your fears

Ask youth how fear can sometimes stop us from doing what is right (e.g. standing up to a bully, stopping someone from backbiting, standing up to peer pressure). Have each person write or draw a symbol on the cracker that represents a fear that prevents them from doing what is right (e.g. fear of being ridiculed, fear of being alienated, etc). On the large freezer bag, have youth write down things that assist them in overcoming their fears (e.g. relying on Allah, thinking positively, remembering a past accomplishment, etc). Place some crackers in the freezer bag then pass around the bag for the youth to take turns crushing their fears. They can each have their own small bag or share one large bag. They can also crush the crackers with their hands or stomp on them. Debrief with the youth on why they chose such fears, how it made them feel and what actions they can take when encountering that fear. (*Supplies: freezer bag, matzah crackers, markers or paint pens*)

Source: Character Council

Read more at *https://masnational.org/1dd*

Let's reflect

1. What do you fear? Why? Which are healthy fears? Unhealthy fears?

2. What are your strengths? If you only think about your weaknesses, will you have the strength to act bravely? How can you use your strengths to develop courage?

3. Share an example of when you displayed courage. Share an example of when you wish you would have displayed courage. Share a time when you saw someone not display courage when they could have.

4. Share examples of using courage in negative ways. Examples: jumping off a roof to impress your friends (true story—the boy broke his leg), vaping, smoking, etc.

5. Share examples of using courage in positive ways. Examples: making a new friend, trying to learn how to rollerblade, taking a class that might be difficult.

6. Don't fear the creation, fear the Creator. What do these words mean to you?

7. The verse below contains some advice on how to be brave. Although it mentions facing the enemy in the battlefield, it can be applied to facing any scary situation. Can you find the prescription? Have you

ever tried this technique? Share your experiences. "O believers! When you face an enemy, stand firm and remember Allah often so you may triumph." (8:45)

8. Who is a famous person you know who displays courage? Who is someone not famous you know who displays courage?

9. Discuss Martin Luther King Jr.'s statement, "The ultimate measure of a person is not where they stand in moments of comfort but where they stand in times of challenge and controversy." Do you agree? Why or why not?

10. Does being brave mean that you don't feel fear? Nelson Mandela said, "I learned that courage was not the absence of fear, but the triumph over it. The brave man is not he who does not feel afraid, but he who conquers that fear." Share examples of a time when you felt afraid, but still persevered and acted with courage.

11. What names and attributes of Allah remind us of the importance of being brave? Discuss how Allah is *Al-Qawiyy* (The Most Strong), *Al-Mateen* (The Firm), and *Al-Qahhar* (The Dominant) and how we can channel those names of Allah in our daily lives.

Let's make dua

1. O Allah! I seek refuge in You from worry and grief, I seek refuge in You from inability and laziness, I seek refuge in You from cowardice and stinginess, and I seek refuge in You from the burden of debt and the tyranny of men. (Abu Dawud)

اللَّهُمَّ إِنِّي أَعُوذُ بكَ مِنَ الهَمِّ والحَزَنِ، وأعوذُ بكَ مِنَ العَجزِ والكَسَلِ، وأعوذُ بكَ مِنَ الجبنِ والبُخلِ، وأعوذُ بكَ مِن غَلَبةِ الدَّينِ وقَهرِ الرجالِ

2. My Lord! Uplift my heart for me, and make my task easy, and remove the impediment from my tongue so people may understand my speech. (20:25-28)

رَبِّ اشْرَحْ لِي صَدْرِي وَيَسِّرْ لِي أَمْرِي وَاحْلُلْ عُقْدَةً مِنْ لِسَانِي يَفْقَهُوا قَوْلِي

3. O Allah, nothing is easy except what You make easy, and You make the difficult easy, if You will. (Ibn Hibban)

اللَّهُمَّ لاَ سَهْلَ إِلاَّ مَا جَعَلتَهُ سَهْلاً، وأَنْتَ تَجْعَلُ الحَزْنَ إِذَا شِئْتَ سَهْلاً

4. In the Name of Allah, Who with His Name nothing can cause harm in the earth nor in the heavens, and He is the All-Hearing, the All-Knowing. "Whoever recites it three times in the morning will not be afflicted by any calamity before evening, and whoever recites it three times in the evening will not be overtaken by any calamity before morning." (Abu Dawud)

بِسمِ اللهِ الذي لا يَضُرُّ مَعَ اسمِهِ شَيءٌ في الأرْضِ وَلا في السّمـــاءِ وَهوَ السّميعُ العَليم

A Scout is Brave

Suggested Curriculum

The content included for each characteristic can span several scouting seasons. In this section, we have included a suggested curriculum for an entire month to simplify your planning. On week 4, we assumed the troop or youth group would participate in a campout or outdoor activity. The next section is a blank curriculum for you to design your own.

Week 1: Introduction to Brave

Open with Quran	2:250, 31:17, 3:200
Youth Talk	Hadith #1
Leader Talk	• Scout Law definition and Islamic perspective • What does it mean again? • What's in it for me?
Closing Dua	Dua #3

Week 2: Fear Only Allah

Open with Quran	5:44
Youth Talk	Hadith #3
Leader Talk	Strength of Two Words
Activity	Courageous Egg
Closing Dua	Dua #3

Week 3: Being Self-reliant

Open with Quran	2:155-156
Youth Talk	Hadith #2
Leader Talk	Let's Reflect #10
Closing Dua	Dua #3

Week 4 Camp: Bringing it All Together

Open with Quran	3:200
Youth Talk	Loud Noise in Madinah
Leader Talk	Standing up to the Byzantine Emperor
Activity	On a Roll
Closing Dua	Dua #3 (After each prayer)
Campfire	Let's Reflect #1, 2, 3, 11

A Scout is Brave

Design your own Curriculum

Week 1:

Open with Quran	
Youth Talk	
Leader Talk	
Activity	
Closing Dua	

Week 2:

Open with Quran	
Youth Talk	
Leader Talk	
Activity	
Closing Dua	

Week 3:

Open with Quran	
Youth Talk	
Leader Talk	
Activity	
Closing Dua	

Week 4 Camp:

Open with Quran	
Youth Talk	
Leader Talk	
Activity	
Closing Dua	
Campfire	

A Scout is Clean

A Scout is clean. Scouts keep their bodies and minds fit. He chooses friends who also live by high standards. He avoids profanity and pornography. He helps keep his home and community clean. A Scout knows there is no kindness or honor in tasteless behavior, such as using profanity or ethnic slurs, or in making fun of someone who has a disability. A Scout avoids that kind of behavior in his words and in his deeds. He keeps his character clean by carefully monitoring what he views on television and the Internet or reads in books and magazines. (The Scout Handbook)

In Islam, cleanliness is regarded as half of our faith and thus Muslims place a high standard on both physical and spiritual cleanliness. In addition to maintaining a clean demeanor, a Muslim filters what he or she consumes, both physically and mentally.

Allah is *At-Tayyib*, The Good and Pure, and *Al-Quddoos*, The Holy. *Al-Quddoos* means Allah is absolutely pure, free from any imperfection and shortcoming. Allah is Good, Pure, and Holy, and He wants us to strive to embody those qualities in our lives for our own benefit.

What do Allah and the Prophet (s) say about being clean?

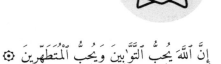

● ● ● ● ● **In the Quran**

إِنَّ ٱللَّهَ يُحِبُّ ٱلتَّوَّٰبِينَ وَيُحِبُّ ٱلْمُتَطَهِّرِينَ ۞

Truly, Allah loves those who turn to Him constantly
and He loves those who keep themselves pure and
clean. (2:222)

قَدْ أَفْلَحَ مَن تَزَكَّىٰ ۞ وَذَكَرَ ٱسْمَ رَبِّهِۦ فَصَلَّىٰ ۞

Successful indeed are those who purify themselves,
remember the Name of their Lord, and pray. (87:14-15)

يَـٰٓأَيُّهَا ٱلَّذِينَ ءَامَنُوا۟ لَا تَتَّبِعُوا۟ خُطُوَٰتِ ٱلشَّيْطَٰنِ وَمَن يَتَّبِعْ خُطُوَٰتِ ٱلشَّيْطَٰنِ
فَإِنَّهُۥ يَأْمُرُ بِٱلْفَحْشَآءِ وَٱلْمُنكَرِ وَلَوْلَا فَضْلُ ٱللَّهِ عَلَيْكُمْ وَرَحْمَتُهُۥ مَا زَكَىٰ مِنكُم
مِّنْ أَحَدٍ أَبَدًا وَلَـٰكِنَّ ٱللَّهَ يُزَكِّى مَن يَشَآءُ وَٱللَّهُ سَمِيعٌ عَلِيمٌ ۞

O believers! Do not follow the footsteps of Satan.
Whoever follows Satan's footsteps, then he surely bids
to immorality and wickedness. Had it not been for Allah's
grace and mercy upon you, none of you would have ever
been purified. But Allah purifies whoever He wills. And
Allah is All-Hearing, All-Knowing. (24:21)

يَٰٓأَيُّهَا ٱلنَّاسُ كُلُوا۟ مِمَّا فِى ٱلْأَرْضِ حَلَٰلًا طَيِّبًا وَلَا تَتَّبِعُوا۟ خُطُوَٰتِ ٱلشَّيْطَٰنِ ۚ إِنَّهُۥ لَكُمْ عَدُوٌّ مُّبِينٌ ۞

O humanity! Eat from what is lawful and good on earth and do not follow Satan's footsteps. He is truly your sworn enemy. (2:168)

لَّمَسْجِدٌ أُسِّسَ عَلَى ٱلتَّقْوَىٰ مِنْ أَوَّلِ يَوْمٍ أَحَقُّ أَن تَقُومَ فِيهِ ۚ فِيهِ رِجَالٌ يُحِبُّونَ أَن يَتَطَهَّرُوا۟ ۚ وَٱللَّهُ يُحِبُّ ٱلْمُطَّهِّرِينَ ۞

...A mosque founded on righteousness from the first day is more worthy of your prayers. In it are men who love to be purified. And Allah loves those who purify themselves. (9:108)

يَٰٓأَيُّهَا ٱلَّذِينَ ءَامَنُوٓا۟ إِذَا قُمْتُمْ إِلَى ٱلصَّلَوٰةِ فَٱغْسِلُوا۟ وُجُوهَكُمْ وَأَيْدِيَكُمْ إِلَى ٱلْمَرَافِقِ وَٱمْسَحُوا۟ بِرُءُوسِكُمْ وَأَرْجُلَكُمْ إِلَى ٱلْكَعْبَيْنِ

You who believe, when you rise up for prayer, wash your faces and your hands as far as the elbows, wipe your heads with wet hands and wash your feet to the ankles... (5:6)

In the Hadith

1. "Cleanliness is half of faith." (Muslim)

2. "Verily, Allah is pure, and He loves purity. He is clean, and He loves cleanliness..." (Tirmithi)

3. "Ten acts are part of *fitrah* (the natural, pure state of human beings): trimming the mustache, letting the beard grow, using the *miswak* (toothstick), sniffing water into the nose, clipping the nails, washing the knuckles, removing hair from the underarms, shaving the pubic hair, and cleaning the private parts with water." Mus'ab said, "I forgot the tenth, except that it might be rinsing the mouth." (Muslim)

4. "Were it not hardship for my nation, I would have obligated them to use the *miswak* (toothstick) at every *wudu* (washing for prayer)." (Malik)

5. "Whoever takes a bath on a Friday and does it well, purifies himself and does it well, puts on his best clothes, and puts on whatever Allah decrees for him of the perfume of his family, then comes to the mosque and does not engage in idle talk or separate between two people; he will be forgiven for his sins between that day and the previous Friday." (Ibn Majah)

6. "Beware of the three acts that cause you to be cursed: relieving yourselves in shaded places (that people utilize), upon a walkway, or in a watering place." (Al-Albani)

7. "Verily, I am only like a father to you in the way that I teach you. When one of you goes to relieve himself, he should not face the direction of prayer or turn his back to it completely, and he should not cleanse himself with his right hand." (Abu Dawud)

8. "While a man was walking along a path, he found a thorny branch of a tree on the way and removed it. Allah thanked him for that deed and forgave him." (Bukhari)

9. Someone asked the Prophet (s), "Which of the people is best?" He said, "Everyone who is pure of heart and sincere in speech." The Companions asked, "Sincere in speech, we understand, but what is pure of heart?" He (s) said, "It is the heart that is pious and pure, with no sin, injustice, rancor or envy in it."

10. Ibn Abbas reported that a beautiful woman would pray in the congregation behind the Messenger of Allah (s). Some men would come early to be in the first row, so as not to gaze at her. Some of them would come late to be in the last row, so that when they bowed, they would stare at her from between their limbs. Allah Almighty revealed the verse, "We surely know who comes first among you and We surely know who comes last." (15:24) (Tirmithi)

What does it mean again?

Clean as a whistle. A Muslim maintains a clean body. Allah has entrusted our body to us and we should take care of it and use it to serve Him.

Garbage in, garbage out. A Muslim understands that if we expose our minds to filth, that will impact our actions negatively.

A Muslim keeps their home and room clean. Allah blessed us with a place to live that is also a trust and must be maintained.

Clean Environment. A clean community is free of trash and debris. It's also free from drugs and other things that harm people.

Clean mind and heart. A Muslim also works to keep their mind and heart clean from harmful ideas and images.

Clean Consumer. A Muslim consumes only what is halal in their food, livelihood, and everything else.

 *Tell Me A Story*

• • • **Mystery of the Man of Paradise**
Ibn Umar hatches a plan to find out why one man was so special. (pg. 246)

• • • **The Woman who Cleaned the Mosque**
The Prophet (s) honored Umm Mihjan and gave her special attention. (pg. 248)

Earning Allah's love. Allah loves His servants who keep themselves clean and pure.

A healthier life. By maintaining clean habits and washing oneself regularly, you are less likely to get sick and suffer from allergies.

Promotes mental clarity and focus. A clean workspace declutters your mind and enables you to stay focused on the task at hand.

Positivity and confidence. Looking polished and smelling pleasant exudes confidence when you walk into a room or interview.

Less anxiety and stress. Clutter is viewed as unfinished business, and this lack of completion is unsettling and stressful to most people.

Better productivity. A clean home and workspace enables you to be more productive as you spend less time searching for things and more time doing.

Less pollution. Contributing to a clean environment means you will have healthier air to breathe, cleaner soil, better food to eat and more pleasant sights to see.

Let's do this

• • • Clean up your Act

At the beginning of a meeting or campout, use a UV marker to mark everyone's hands in several places or brush their hands with water mixed with highlighter ink without telling them what it is for. After activities or before mealtime, all youth should wash their hands. When everyone gets back together, explain that everyone will put their hands under a UV light to see how clean their hands are. The UV marker represents hidden germs and filth that may remain on our hands if we don't wash them thoroughly. The person leading the activity can give instructions on how to wash hands properly and invite youth to repeat the washing, if needed. (*Supplies: paint brush, disposable gloves, disposable container, UV torch or lamp, highlighter pen*) **Source: Scouts.org**

Read more at *https://masnational.org/ckp*

• • • The 5S Framework

Use the 5S system to organize your patrol box or shed. This method is used in factories, workplaces, and other professional settings. 5S stands for: Sort, Set in order, Shine, Standardize, Sustain. Spread this activity out over several weeks. **Source: 5S Today**

Read more at *https://masnational.org/4k9*

• • • Uniform Inspection

At the beginning of the troop meeting, have the patrol leaders examine the uniforms of their members and comment on how they can be improved.

• • • 3 Bucket Method

Teach the 3 Bucket Method (Wash, Rinse, Sanitize) to clean dishes at a campout. (*Details on this method can be found in the Scout Handbook.*) **Source: On Scouting magazine**

Read more at *https://masnational.org/7ln*

Let's reflect

1. Why do you think Allah commands us to make *wudu* (washing for prayer) before prayer?

2. What is the biggest challenge in keeping a clean room? What can you do about it?

3. "Everything has a place, and everything is in its place." How does that mindset contribute to being clean?

4. What are the daily activities you should be doing to keep clean? What habits should you be doing every few days, week, and month in personal hygiene?

5. What do you do with your gear when you return from a camping trip?

6. How do you clean after relieving yourself in the wilderness?

7. Why should we sit down when we use the restroom?

8. Allah has entrusted us with many things including our body, clothes, etc. How does cleanliness relate to respecting Allah and His creations?

9. How do you maintain a clean mind and clean thoughts?

10. What names and attributes of Allah remind us of the importance of being clean? Discuss how Allah is *Al-Quddoos* (The Pure) and *At-Tayyib* (The Good) and how we can channel those names of Allah in our daily lives.

Let's make dua

1. *Dua* after *wudu*: O Allah, make me of those who return to you often in repentance, and make me of those who remain pure and clean. (Tirmithi)

اللّهُمَّ اجْعَلْنِي مِنَ التَّوَّابِينَ ، وَاجْعَلْنِي مِنَ الْمُتَطَهِّرِينَ

2. *Dua* upon beginning the prayer: O Allah, distance me from my sins just as You have distanced The East from The West. O Allah, purify me of my sins as a white robe is purified of filth. O Allah, cleanse me of my sins with snow, water, and ice. (Bukhari)

اللّهُمَّ بَاعِدْ بَيْنِي وَبَيْنَ خَطَايَايَ كَمَا بَاعَدْتَ بَيْنَ الْمَشْرِقِ وَالْمَغْرِبِ، اللّهُمَّ نَقِّنِي مِنْ خَطَايَايَ كَمَا يُنَقَّى الثَّوْبُ الأَبْيَضُ مِنَ الدَّنَسِ، اللّهُمَّ اغْسِلْنِي مِنْ خَطَايَايَ بِالْمَاءِ وَالثَّلْجِ وَالْبَرَدِ

3. *Dua* upon entering the bathroom: O Allah, I seek protection in You from evil, impure beings and deeds. (Bukhari)

االلّهُمَّ إِنِّي أَعُوذُ بِكَ مِنَ الْخُبُثِ وَالْخَبَائِثِ

Let's teach it

A Scout is Clean

Suggested Curriculum

The content included for each characteristic can span several scouting seasons. In this section, we have included a suggested curriculum for an entire month to simplify your planning. On week 4, we assumed the troop or youth group would participate in a campout or outdoor activity. The next section is a blank curriculum for you to design your own.

Week 1: Introduction to Clean

Open with Quran	2:222
Youth Talk	Hadith #1, 2
Leader Talk	• Scout Law definition and Islamic perspective • What does it mean again? • What's in it for me?
Activity	Let's Reflect #4
Closing Dua	Dua #1

Week 2: Clean Body

Open with Quran	87:14–15
Leader Talk	The Woman who Cleaned the Mosque
Activity	Uniform Inspection
Closing Dua	Dua #1

Week 3: Clean Mind & Heart

Open with Quran	24:21
Youth Talk	Hadith #9
Leader Talk	Mystery of the Man of Paradise
Activity	Let's Reflect #9
Closing Dua	Dua #1

Week 4 Camp: Bringing it All Together

Open with Quran	9:108
Youth Talk	• What's in it for me? • Let's Reflect #10
Leader Talk	Hadith #3
Activity	• *Wudu* Workshop • Clean Up Your Act
Closing Dua	Dua #1 (After each prayer)
Campfire	Let's Reflect #1

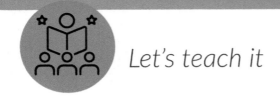

Let's teach it

A Scout is Clean

Design your own Curriculum

Week 1:

Open with Quran	
Youth Talk	
Leader Talk	
Activity	
Closing Dua	

Week 2:

Open with Quran	
Youth Talk	
Leader Talk	
Activity	
Closing Dua	

Week 3:

Open with Quran	
Youth Talk	
Leader Talk	
Activity	
Closing Dua	

Week 4 Camp:

Open with Quran	
Youth Talk	
Leader Talk	
Activity	
Closing Dua	
Campfire	

A Scout is Reverent

A Scout is reverent. A Scout is reverent toward God. He is faithful in his religious duties. He respects the beliefs of others. Wonders all around us remind us of our faith in God, and we show our reverence by living our lives according to the ideals of our beliefs. You will encounter people expressing their reverence in many ways. It is your duty to respect and defend their rights to their religious beliefs even when they differ from your own. (The Scout Handbook)

The Muslim is in awe of Allah and seeks to please Him by following His commands and staying away from His prohibitions. In Islam, there is no compulsion in religion, and the Muslim respects others' beliefs while staying true to his or her own way of life. A Muslim realizes that everything in nature praises and submits to Allah; this should evoke a sense of reverence. Muslims also give special reverence to the Prophet (s), following his example and praying for peace upon him whenever he is mentioned.

Allah is *Al-Khaaliq*, The Creator. *Al-Khaaliq* created everything from nothing. He created the earth with its oceans, mountains, and deserts. He created humans and animals as well as creatures of the unseen. He created cells, atoms, forests and galaxies. He is *Al-Aliyy* (The Most High) and *Al-Kabeer* (The Great). When the Muslim says *Allahu Akbar* (God is the Greatest), in prayer or outside of prayer, he or she says it with reverence, knowing that God is greater than anything we can imagine.

What do Allah and the Prophet (s) say about being reverent?

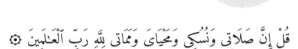

In the Quran

قُلْ إِنَّ صَلَاتِى وَنُسُكِى وَمَحْيَاىَ وَمَمَاتِى لِلَّهِ رَبِّ ٱلْعَٰلَمِينَ ۝

Say, 'Surely, my prayer and my devotion, my life and my death are all for Allah, the Lord of the Worlds.' (6:162)

إِنَّمَا ٱلْمُؤْمِنُونَ ٱلَّذِينَ إِذَا ذُكِرَ ٱللَّهُ وَجِلَتْ قُلُوبُهُمْ وَإِذَا تُلِيَتْ عَلَيْهِمْ ءَايَٰتُهُۥ زَادَتْهُمْ إِيمَٰنًا وَعَلَىٰ رَبِّهِمْ يَتَوَكَّلُونَ ۝

The true believers are those whose hearts tremble at the remembrance of Allah, whose faith increases when His revelations are recited to them, and who put their trust in their Lord. (8:2)

إِنَّ ٱلَّذِينَ ءَامَنُواْ وَعَمِلُواْ ٱلصَّٰلِحَٰتِ وَأَقَامُواْ ٱلصَّلَوٰةَ وَءَاتَوُاْ ٱلزَّكَوٰةَ لَهُمْ أَجْرُهُمْ عِندَ رَبِّهِمْ وَلَا خَوْفٌ عَلَيْهِمْ وَلَا هُمْ يَحْزَنُونَ ۝

Those who believe and do good deeds, establish prayers, and give charity, will have their reward with their Lord, and there will be no fear concerning them, nor will they grieve. (2:277)

خَلَقَ ٱلسَّمَـٰوَٰتِ بِغَيْرِ عَمَدٍ تَرَوْنَهَا ۖ وَأَلْقَىٰ فِي ٱلْأَرْضِ رَوَٰسِيَ أَن تَمِيدَ بِكُمْ وَبَثَّ فِيهَا مِن كُلِّ دَآبَّةٍ ۚ وَأَنزَلْنَا مِنَ ٱلسَّمَآءِ مَآءً فَأَنۢبَتْنَا فِيهَا مِن كُلِّ زَوْجٍ كَرِيمٍ ۝

He created the heavens without pillars as you see them, and put mountains upon the Earth lest it might convulse with you, and He spread it with animals of all kinds; and We sent down water from the clouds, then caused to grow therein (vegetation) of every noble kind. (31:10)

إِنَّ ٱللَّهَ وَمَلَـٰٓئِكَتَهُۥ يُصَلُّونَ عَلَى ٱلنَّبِىِّ ۚ يَـٰٓأَيُّهَا ٱلَّذِينَ ءَامَنُوا۟ صَلُّوا۟ عَلَيْهِ وَسَلِّمُوا۟ تَسْلِيمًا ۝

Indeed, Allah showers His blessings upon the Prophet, and His angels pray for him. O believers! Invoke Allah's blessings upon him, and salute him with worthy greetings of peace. (33:56)

لَآ إِكْرَاهَ فِي ٱلدِّينِ ۖ قَد تَّبَيَّنَ ٱلرُّشْدُ مِنَ ٱلْغَىِّ ۚ فَمَن يَكْفُرْ بِٱلطَّـٰغُوتِ وَيُؤْمِنۢ بِٱللَّهِ فَقَدِ ٱسْتَمْسَكَ بِٱلْعُرْوَةِ ٱلْوُثْقَىٰ لَا ٱنفِصَامَ لَهَا ۗ وَٱللَّهُ سَمِيعٌ عَلِيمٌ ۝

There is no compulsion in religion: true guidance has become distinct from error, so whoever rejects false gods and believes in Allah has grasped the firmest handhold, one that will never break. Allah is All-Hearing and All-Knowing. (2:256)

• • • In the Hadith

1. The Prophet (s) would seek refuge in Allah from four things: from knowledge that does not benefit, from a heart without reverence, from a supplication that is unanswered, and from an ego that is never satisfied. (an-Nasa'i)

2. "The first thing to be removed from this nation will be reverence, until you will not see anyone with reverence." (Al-Albani)

3. "Islam has been built on five [pillars]: testifying that there is no deity worthy of worship except Allah and that Muhammad is the Messenger of Allah, establishing the prayer, paying the *zakah*, making the *hajj* to the House, and fasting in Ramadan." (Bukhari & Muslim)

4. "Reflect deeply upon the creation, but do not reflect upon the essence of the Creator. Verily, His essence cannot be known other than to believe in it." (al-Albani)

5. The Prophet (s) said that Allah says, "Son of Adam, so long as you call upon Me, and hope in Me, I shall forgive you for what you have done, and I shall not mind. Son of Adam, were your sins to reach the clouds in the sky and were you then to ask forgiveness of Me, I shall forgive you. Son of Adam, were you to come to Me with an earthful of sins and were you then to face Me, without having

worshiped anything with Me, I shall grant you an earthful of pardon." (Tirmithi)

6. "Beware! Whoever is cruel and hard on a non-Muslim minority, curtails their rights, burdens them with more than they can bear, or takes anything from them against their free will, I (Prophet Muhammad) will complain against the person on the Day of Judgment." (Abu Dawud)

What does it mean again?

Recognize the awesomeness of Allah. A Muslim looks at his or her outside surroundings differently, knowing that all of what they see demonstrates the glory of Allah.

A Muslim feels special reverence towards the Prophet (s). We hold the Prophet (s) in high regard by sending peace and blessings upon him and following his example and Sunnah.

A Muslim is consistent and faithful in their religious obligations. A Muslim is disciplined in adhering to the pillars of their faith and constantly strives to grow closer to Allah.

Respects the beliefs of others. To disrespect or insult another's beliefs is contrary to Islam.

Tell Me A Story

Friendship with Allah. Allah says, "I am near to My servant, and I am with him when he thinks of Me... When he comes to Me walking, I come to him running." (Bukhari) Who wouldn't want to be close to Allah?

Ten Bonus Points! For sending peace and blessings upon the Prophet (s), Allah sends ten blessings upon you, removes ten sins, and raises you ten degrees. (Albani)

Keeps you from sins. Reverence helps you fulfill your religious obligations and keeps you away from sin. Moreover, performing your religious duties grants you many opportunities to remove sins from your scale and, in turn, increases your reverence even more.

Peace of mind. When you are striving to be a righteous Muslim, Allah will find a way out of your difficulties.

Respect. When you respect your own faith and that of others, people will respect you and take you seriously.

Purposeful Living. When you are reverent and focused in your worship and good deeds, you remain focused on the goal and reap the full benefits of your actions.

Let's do this

● ● ● Silent Reflection Hike

Go on a silent hike and reflect on Allah's creations. Hike to a location that evokes a sense of wonder (a mountain, seashore, or watching the sunrise or stars). Encourage the youth to be quiet and reflect for 10 minutes on Allah and His creation. Recite some verses that evoke a sense of awe of Allah. (Surah *al-Mulk*, for example)

● ● ● Earn a Religious Emblem

Pursue the religious emblem such as the 'In the Name of God' from the scouting website.

● ● ● Ten Commandments Hike

Organize a hike with a troop from a different faith to visit each other's religious institution.

● ● ● Shared Service Activity

Organize a service activity with a group from a different faith.

● ● ● Salah Workshop

Conduct a prayer & *wudu* workshop so youth can learn how to pray properly.

• • • Perfect Your Prayer Challenge

Can you practice praying like Hatim al-Asamm?
Read over the following descriptions and then pray a
prayer together that resembles the prayer of Hatim.
Hatim lived at the time of Imam Abu Hanifah; he was
a young man who was known for his knowledge and
worship. Once Hatim al-Asamm was asked how to pray
with reverence. This was his answer: "I establish the
command for prayer and approach with reverence. I
begin prayer with intention and say the takbeer with
awe. I recite with measured recitation and reflection,
bow with reverence, and prostrate with humility. I
then sit to complete the testimony, and I invoke peace
properly and according to the Sunnah. With sincerity,
I surrender the prayer to Allah Almighty. At the same
time, I return to myself with fear that the prayer might
not be accepted from me. I guard my prayer in this
way until death." On another occasion, Hatim said also,
"When I stand up to perform my prayer, I visualize the
Kabah before me, the bridge over Hell beneath my feet,
Paradise to my right and Hell to my left, and the Angel
of Death behind me, fearing all the while that this is
my final prayer. And so I stand between hope and fear."
(Hilyat al-Awliyā' 11623)

Let's reflect

1. Why do you think Allah commands us to pray 5 times a day? How does it shape our life?

2. Do you think Islam has a lot of rules? Why or why not?

3. What does it look like to disrespect someone's beliefs? What are the consequences of disrespecting someone's beliefs? What are some ways that we show respect and consideration for others' beliefs?

4. Think about this verse: "The seven heavens, the earth, and all those in them glorify Him. There is not a single thing that does not glorify His praises—but you simply cannot comprehend their glorification. He is indeed Most Forbearing, All-Forgiving." (17:44) Allah tells us that every creature and form of creation has a way of glorifying Allah. Can you imagine what some of those forms of glorification might be? How does a tree glorify Allah? A cricket? The wind or a star? Do you think we can hear or see some of those forms of glorification, even if we can't understand them?

5. What names and attributes of Allah remind us of the importance of being reverent? Discuss how Allah is *Al-Waahid* (The One), *Al-Ahad* (The Only One), *Al-Khaaliq* (The Creator), *Al-Qahhar* (The Ever-Dominating) and how we can channel those names of Allah in our daily lives.

Let's make dua

1. O Allah, I seek refuge in You from knowledge that does not benefit, from a heart that is not reverent, from a soul that is not content, and from a supplication that is not answered." (Muslim)

اللَّهُمَّ إِنِّي أَعُوذُ بِكَ مِنْ عِلْمٍ لاَ يَنْفَعُ وَمِنْ قَلْبٍ لاَ يَخْشَعُ وَمِنْ نَفْسٍ لاَ تَشْبَعُ وَمِنْ دُعَاءٍ لاَ يُسْمَعُ

2. My Lord! Inspire me to always be thankful for Your favors which You have blessed me and my parents with, and to do good deeds that please You. Admit me, by Your mercy, into [the ranks of] Your righteous servants. (27:19)

رَبِّ أَوْزِعْنِي أَنْ أَشْكُرَ نِعْمَتَكَ ٱلَّتِي أَنْعَمْتَ عَلَيَّ وَعَلَى وَالِدَيَّ وَأَنْ أَعْمَلَ صَٰلِحًا تَرْضَٰهُ وَأَدْخِلْنِي بِرَحْمَتِكَ فِي عِبَادِكَ ٱلصَّٰلِحِينَ

3. O Allah, I seek refuge in You lest I worship anything with You knowingly, and I seek Your forgiveness for what I know not. (Albani)

اللَّهُمَّ إِنِّي أَعُوذُ بِكَ أَنْ أُشْرِكَ بِكَ وَأَنَا أَعْلَمُ، وَأَسْتَغْفِرُكَ لِمَا لاَ أَعْلَمُ

4. O Allah, apportion to us enough fear as should serve as a barrier between us and acts of disobedience; and apportion to us enough obedience as will take us to Your Paradise, and such conviction as will make it easy for us to bear the calamities of this world. (Tirmithi)

اللَّهُمَّ اقْسِمْ لَنَا مِنْ خَشْيَتِكَ مَا تَحُولُ بِهِ بَيْنَنَا وَبَيْنَ مَعَاصِيكَ، وَمِنْ طَاعَتِكَ مَا تُبَلِّغُنَا بِهِ جَنَّتَكَ، وَمِنَ الْيَقِينِ مَا تُهَوِّنُ بِهِ عَلَيْنَا مَصَائِبَ الدُّنْيَا

Let's teach it

A Scout is Reverent

Suggested Curriculum

The content included for each characteristic can span several scouting seasons. In this section, we have included a suggested curriculum for an entire month to simplify your planning. On week 4, we assumed the troop or youth group would participate in a campout or outdoor activity. The next section is a blank curriculum for you to design your own.

Week 1: Introduction to Reverent

Open with Quran	2:195 11:29
Youth Talk	Hadith #5
Leader Talk	• Introduction to Being Reverent • Scout Law definition and Islamic perspective • What does it mean again?
Closing Dua	Dua #1

Week 2: Reverence to Allah

Open with Quran	31:10 8:2
Youth Talk	Hadith #1
Leader Talk	The Weeping Tree
Activity	Salah Workshop
Closing Dua	Dua #1

Week 3: Faithful to Your Religious Duties

Open with Quran	2:277 6:162
Youth Talk	Hadith #3
Leader Talk	The Mindful Milkmaid
Closing Dua	Dua #1

Week 4 Camp: Bringing it All Together

Open with Quran	2:256
Youth Talk	• Hadith #6 • What's in it for me?
Leader Talk	Standing for a Jewish Funeral
Activity	• Silent Reflection Hike • Let's Reflect #4
Closing Dua	Dua #1 (After each prayer)
Campfire	Let's Reflect #3

Let's teach it

A Scout is Reverent

Design your own Curriculum

Week 1:

Open with Quran	
Youth Talk	
Leader Talk	
Activity	
Closing Dua	

Week 2:

Open with Quran	
Youth Talk	
Leader Talk	
Activity	
Closing Dua	

Week 3:

Open with Quran	
Youth Talk	
Leader Talk	
Activity	
Closing Dua	

Week 4 Camp:

Open with Quran	
Youth Talk	
Leader Talk	
Activity	
Closing Dua	
Campfire	

A Scout is ...

TRUSTWORTHY

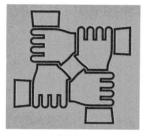

LOYAL

HELPFUL

FRIENDLY

COURTEOUS

KIND

OBEDIENT

CHEERFUL

THRIFTY

BRAVE

CLEAN

REVERENT

• • • A Trustworthy Tax Return

While Abu Ubayda was the commander of the Muslim
armies in Syria, the Emperor of Byzantium set out with
a large army to recapture the city of Homs. Abu Ubayda
decided to evacuate because he had only a handful of
soldiers and could not effectively defend the city. He
gathered the people of Homs in the middle of the city
and announced, "We collected the protection tax from
you because we planned to defend you and maintain
your city. Now we are too weak, and so we return to
you the tax we collected." All the taxes collected were
returned to the non-Muslim people of Homs before the
Muslims withdrew from the city.

• • • A Shining Reputation

In the early stages of his Prophethood, Prophet
Muhammad (s) gathered all the people of Mecca and
asked them, "O people of Mecca! If I say that an army
is advancing on you from behind the mountains, would
you believe me?" All said in one voice, "Yes, because we
have never heard you telling a lie!" All the people, without

exception, swore to his truthfulness because he had lived an honest, trustworthy life among them for forty years. His nickname among the people of Makkah was *as-Sadiq al-Amin* (the truthful and trustworthy).

Many years later, as he (s) was preparing to flee Makkah and migrate to Madinah, he left behind his cousin Ali ibn Abi Talib to take care of one last task. You see, although the people of Makkah persecuted and ridiculed the Prophet (s), they still trusted him so much that they kept their personal valuables in his home. Even though the Prophet (s) was fleeing for his life, he left behind Ali to make sure all of the entrusted valuables were returned to their owners.

• • • The Repentant Robber

Abdulqadir Jilani was a great scholar of Islam, born in 11th-century Persia. There is a story about him as a boy, before he became a scholar, that illustrates his unconditional truthfulness. Abdulqadir's mother wanted her son to become a scholar, so she prepared him for a long journey to Baghdad where he would study under the greatest teachers of the time. Before her son departed, she did two things. She stitched 40 dinars into the lining of his clothing so that they would not be easily found by thieves. Then she advised her son to always tell the truth. She quoted the hadith of the Prophet (s), "Truthfulness leads to righteousness and righteousness leads to Paradise..." and the verse of the Quran, "O you who believe! Be careful of your duty to God, and be with the truthful." (9:119)

En route to Baghdad, Abdulqadir's caravan was attacked by highway robbers. They searched each traveler one by one, stripping them of their money and valuables. When they came upon Abdulqadir, they asked him, "Do you have any money?" Abdulqadir remembered the words of his mother and answered calmly, "Yes." The bandits searched the boy, but could not find anything. They took the boy to their leader, who found the 40 gold dinars in the lining of his coat.

Impressed by the boy's insistence on telling the truth, he asked the boy who he was and where he was going. Abdulqadir told him he was going to study under the scholars. When the robber inquired why he didn't hide his coins, Abdulqadir answered with the words of his mother—the hadith and the verse of the Quran. The robbers were astounded by the young man's determination to tell the truth and returned the money to the travelers. It is said that the leader of the robbers later traveled to Baghdad and would become one of Abdulqadir's students.

• • • A Truthful Reporter

There was some trouble brewing in Madinah. Two men, one from the Ansar and one from the Muhajirun, had an argument. This argument divided many people in the city, with the Ansar taking one side and the Muhajirun taking the other. The Prophet (s) intervened, telling people to remember the brotherhood between them and not engage in small disputes that did not concern them.

The leader of the hypocrites, Abdullah ibn Ubayy, however, would not let the issue go. Even after the Prophet (s) called the believers to stop, Abdullah ibn Ubayy tried to revive the tension by encouraging the Ansar to be angry at the newcomers to Madinah, the Muhajirun. A young boy named Zaid ibn Arqam was present while Abdullah ibn Ubayy was attempting to rile up the Ansar. He went and informed his uncle of what had been said. His uncle then went and informed the Prophet (s).

The Prophet (s) summoned Abdullah ibn Ubayy who pretended to be indignant and surprised. He would never say such things! He was loyal to the Prophet (s) and wished no trouble! Who had made those claims against them? A young boy? Surely, the Prophet (s) wouldn't take the word of a young boy over a noble, grown man?

Not wanting to continue to hear the weak defenses of this hypocrite, the Prophet (s) sent him away. Zaid watched the man storm out of the Prophet's company. Because the Prophet (s) did not have proof he could not take any action, and this was difficult for Zaid to understand. He felt that the Prophet (s) did not believe him. He ran away, crying.

Soon the Prophet (s) called him back, gently sat the boy in front of him and recited to him some newly revealed verses of the Quran (*Surah al-Munafiqun*). These verses had been revealed to expose Abdullah ibn Ubayy and to affirm what Zaid had reported. Zaid was the first to hear those verses upon revelation. Imagine how special he must have felt to have his report confirmed by Allah!

● ● ● High and Low Company

Once the wealthy nobles of Quraish came to the Prophet (s). They told him that if only the poor and downtrodden Muslims would go away and leave the Prophet's company, they would be more willing to listen to his message. The nobles said, "We are willing to listen to you, but we are noble and wealthy people. We cannot sit with the likes of these people."

Many of the early Muslims were poor and from the lower classes of Makkan society. Some of them were even slaves. Ammar ibn Yassir and his family were originally from Yemen, but poverty had forced them to serve as slaves in Makkah. Suhaib ar-Rumi was a fair-skinned man who escaped slavery in the Byzantine Empire and who was often appointed to represent the Quraish merchants. Bilal ibn Rabah was the Abyssinian slave who was freed by Abu Bakr after being horribly tortured by Quraish leaders. Abdullah ibn Masud, who would become one of the greatest scholars of the Quran, was the child of slaves. These were some of the Companions of the Prophet (s) with whom Quraish did not want to be associated or even found in the same gathering.

Allah emphasized to the Prophet (s) to remain loyal to these early Muslims, regardless of their social status or past. In *Surah al-Kahf* verse 28, Allah commanded the Prophet (s) never to turn away from the believers.

• • • Loyalty to Khadijah

The Prophet (s) was loyal to his beloved wife Khadijah long after she passed away. Many years after her death, Khadijah's sister, Hala bint Khuwaylid, came to visit the Prophet (s). When the Prophet (s) heard her voice, he was overjoyed because it reminded him of his late wife. Aisha became jealous and commented, "Khadijah was just an old woman of Quraish, and Allah has given you someone better than her." The Prophet (s) was dearly loyal to Khadijah, even after her death, and would not let anyone, even his beloved Aisha, say anything negative about her. He (s) responded, "Allah has not replaced her with someone better. She believed in me when people rejected me, she saw me as truthful when others called me a liar, she supported me with her wealth when others denied me, and Allah blessed me with children from her and not from others."

• • • Youth of the Cave

In *Surah al-Kahf*, Allah tells us the story of a group of young people who decided that their loyalty to Allah was greater than their loyalty to their families and city. Because their city would not allow them to practice their faith, they separated themselves, leaving behind their homes and wealth and retreating to a cave in the mountains. As young men, they left behind many opportunities and privileges. They fled to the cave where they hoped to be safe with their most valuable possession —their faith in Allah. Their story is one of deep sacrifice, loyalty, and profound belief in Allah. It is important to remember that the Sunnah of the Prophet (s) encourages remaining among our people and not withdrawing from community, but in this case, the youth were so persecuted that they could not cling to their faith unless they fled.

● ● ● Better than Fasting!

Anas ibn Malik narrated that the Prophet (s) and his Companions were on a journey, and some of the Companions were fasting while others were not. The weather was extremely hot, and so those who were fasting struggled to perform the chores of feeding the animals and preparing the food. So the Companions who were not fasting performed these tasks for them. Although fasting is an act that is extremely pleasing to Allah, the Prophet (s) said of their situation: "Those who were not fasting took all of the reward today." (Bukhari and Muslim)

● ● ● Better than *Itikaaf*!

Ibn Abbas was once making *itikaaf* (a time of seclusion) in the Prophet's mosque. A man approached him and sat down with him. Ibn Abbas said, "My friend, you seem sad and troubled!" The man replied, "Yes, cousin of the Prophet. I am really in trouble. I owe a lot of money, and by the grave of the Prophet (s), I can't repay it." Ibn Abbas asked, "What if I speak with your creditor?" The man said, "If you wish to."

So Ibn Abbas got up, put on his shoes, and proceeded to leave the mosque. The man, seeing this, exclaimed, "Have you forgotten that you are in *itikaaf*?" Ibn Abbas responded, "No, I haven't forgotten. But still fresh in my mind are the words of the one who lies in this grave saying with his eyes full of tears, "Whoever sets forth in the service of his brother and settles an affair for him, that is better than ten years of *itikaaf*. And for just one day of truly seeking Allah's pleasure in *itikaaf*, Allah will spread three trenches between him and the fire of Hell, the width of each trench being greater than the distance between the Heaven and the earth." (al-Hakim & at-Tabarani)

● ● ● The Most Difficult Job

When the Muslims of Madinah found out their city was about to be attacked by several armies, they only had a few days to decide on a strategy. They made the decision to construct a massive trench on the exposed side of their city. The trench was to be 3 miles long, 16 feet deep, and 20 feet wide – and they only had six days to dig it. Everyone helped. People dug, prepared food, managed the teams, carried water, broke the large rocks, and hauled small rocks out of the ditch. What job do you think the Prophet (s) did? He volunteered for the most difficult and tedious job–hauling the dirt out of the deep trench. By doing the most tedious job, he was being of the greatest benefit and help to his people.

• • • Umar Bakes the Bread

Ibn Abbas related this story which happened while he accompanied the Caliph Umar on a cold night making his rounds of the tents and houses of the poor, making sure all of their needs are met. He said: When we were about to head back, we noticed a tent in which there was an old woman, and around her were some children crying. In front of her was a fireplace on which rested a cooking pot, under which a fire was burning. She kept saying to the children. "Hush! Hush my children, in a little while, the food will be cooked, and you shall eat."

We stood at a distance from the spot, and Umar observed silently, gazing sometimes at the old woman and other times at the children. We stood that way for a long time. Then I said to him, "O leader of the believers! Why are you standing in this way? Let us return." He replied, "By God! I will not leave until I have seen her pour food from the pot, and her children have eaten and are satisfied." We stood there for a very long time and grew restless. Meanwhile, the children continued crying, and the old woman kept telling them the food would be ready soon.

Finally we approached her. Umar said to her, "Assalam alaikum my Aunt!" and she returned his salutation warmly. He asked her, 'Why are these children crying and weeping?' She replied, "Because they are so hungry." Umar said, "Why don't you feed them what is in the pot?" She replied, "What is there in the pot that I should feed them? It is only to divert their attention until they get weary of crying, and sleep overcomes them, for I have nothing to feed them with."

Umar walked over to the pot and found that it contained small pebbles with water boiling over them. He was surprised and asked her why there were only rocks. She replied, "I make them imagine that there is something being cooked in the pot and hope it is enough to distract them until they get tired and eventually fall asleep." Umar questioned her further and discovered that the woman had no one to help or support her. He told her to wait just a little longer, for they would return soon.

We immediately left the house and returned with flour, ghee and dates. The journey back to the tent was long, and Umar insisted on carrying the heavy sacks on his back, flour spilling onto his face and beard. We arrived panting at the house, hurrying lest the children sleep without food. Umar went in and found the fire had almost gone out. He dropped to the ground, blowing on the fire and adding firewood, and placing a pot with ghee on the fire. Umar stirred the ghee with one hand and began mixing the dough with the other. When the food was ready, Umar served the children until they had their fill and were smiling and playing.

• • • Three Best Friends

There once lived three men who were the very best of friends. They enjoyed each other's company and told one another their deepest secrets. Even better, their friendship was based on seeking the pleasure of Allah and competing in doing good. One of the three friends, al-Waqidi, was a great scholar at the time of the Abbasid Caliph Mamun Rashid. He narrates this incredible story about the three best friends:

I had two friends, one of whom was from the tribe of Banu Hashim. Our friendship was so sincere that it was as though we were three bodies with one soul! One year, as Eid approached, I had no money at all. My wife said to me, "You and I can tolerate not having money. But our kids—they see other children wearing new clothes and receiving gifts, while they get nothing. See if you can get some money so that I can make new clothes for them."

Al-Waqidi wasn't sure what to do, but decided to try writing a letter to his beloved friend from Banu Hashim, asking for some money. The response was quick—the friend from Banu Hashim sent a letter with a sealed bag containing a generous 1,000 dirhams. But before al-Waqidi could open the bag, he received news that the third friend had so much financial difficulty and was in need of help. Without hesitation and before he even laid eyes on the money sent to him from his Banu Hashim friend, al-Waqidi forwarded the sealed bag of 1,000 dirhams to the third friend.

Al-Waqidi went to the mosque with a heavy heart, wondering what he would say to his wife. Ashamed to face her empty-handed, he spent the night in the mosque. He went home in the morning and told his wife what happened. She smiled gently, telling her husband that she was proud of him for putting his friends' needs above his own. Later that day, the friend from Banu Hashim arrived at al-Waqidi's house. Something was troubling him. He asked curiously, "Tell me the truth, al-Waqidi. What did you really do with the bag of money I sent you?" Al-Waqidi told him the whole story.

The friend from Banu Hashim bowed his head for a moment, then explained that yesterday he had sent his final remaining 1,000 dirhams to al-Waqidi to help him. Left with no money himself, he requested money from their third friend. "Imagine my surprise when I received the exact sealed bag I had sent earlier to you!" Realizing together that they were all in need and the same bag of money had passed between all three of their hands, the friends divided the 1,000 dirhams equally between them, and al-Waqidi gave his wife 100 dirhams to make clothing for their children. This incredible story reached the Abbasid Caliph Mamun Rashid, who sent 2,000 gold dinars to each friend, with an extra 1,000 gold dinars as a gift to al-Waqidi's wife.

• • • The Traveling Friend

In a hadith, Prophet Muhammad (s) told us a story about a man who went on a trip. He traveled through the desert, making his way towards another town. Allah sent an angel to question the traveler. The angel asked, "Where are you going?" The man answered, "I am going to visit my brother in another town." The angel asked, "Did you do something for your brother for which you expect some kind of repayment for it?" "No. I am going because I love him for the sake of Allah, The Exalted." Upon these words, the angel announced, "I am a messenger to you from Allah, to inform you that Allah loves you as you love him." (Muslim)

Abu Bakr, True Friend and Supporter

When Prophet Muhammad (s) was a young man, before he became a prophet, he married Khadijah and became neighbors with Abu Bakr. Muhammad (s) and Abu Bakr quickly became close friends, finding that they shared many commonalities. Both were traders, and both were exceedingly honest and kind. Both felt revulsion toward the corruption and cruelty that took place in Makkan society, and both avoided worshiping idols. Their friendship would last a lifetime and would sustain the rise of Islam.

When Prophet Muhammad (s) received the first revelation at the age of 40, Abu Bakr, his best friend of many years, was the first adult man to accept Islam. He had no reservations and trusted Muhammad (s) completely. Everyone else had questions and doubts, but not Abu Bakr. He knew in an instant that Muhammad

(s) was indeed Allah's prophet. He had interacted with Muhammad (s) for the past 15 years and knew his honesty and integrity. Eventually Abu Bakr would be given the name *as-Siddeeq*, man of truth, for his instant belief and trust of the Prophet (s).

Abu Bakr immediately got to work. He met with his circle of friends and started to spread the message of Islam. Some of the strongest and noblest Companions accepted Islam at the hand of Abu Bakr in those early days. Prophet Muhammad's message was spread at first in secret, by word of mouth only, because any news of the new religion would enrage the leaders of Makkah. The Prophet (s) hoped to build a base of followers first so that they could support each other and withstand the difficulties ahead. After some time had passed, and almost 40 people had accepted Islam, Abu Bakr asked the Prophet (s) for permission to make the call to Islam public. Prophet Muhammad (s) was reluctant, but Abu Bakr insisted. Finally, Allah revealed the command to make the call to Islam public. Together, the two friends made their way to the Kabah. Abu Bakr stood up and called out in his loudest voice, "There is none worthy of worship but Allah, and Muhammad is his slave and messenger!" In this way, Abu Bakr became the first public speaker for Islam.

• • • A Mistake in the Mosque

Anas Ibn Malik said: "While we were in the mosque
with the Messenger of Allah, a bedouin came and
stood urinating in the mosque. The Companions said,
'Stop it! Stop it!' and were about to attack him. But
the Messenger of Allah (s) said, 'Do not interrupt him;
leave him alone.' So they left him until he had finished
urinating, then the Messenger of Allah (s) called him and
said, 'In these mosques, it is not right to do anything like
urinating or defecating; they are only for remembering
Allah, praying and reading Quran, or words to that
effect.' Then he commanded a man who was there to
bring a bucket of water and throw it over the urine,
and he did so." (Muslim)

• • • The Frazzled Host

When the Prophet (s) first arrived in Madinah, he
needed a place to stay until the masjid and the house
of the Prophet was built. Everyone wanted to host the
Prophet of Allah, but the honor went to Abu Ayyub
al-Ansari and his family.

Abu Ayyub's house had two floors. He and his wife cleaned and cleared the second floor, reasoning that it was more courteous that the Prophet (s) be above them, not below them. The Prophet (s) requested the lower floor instead, since he would have many guests coming and going during his stay and preferred to be near the door. This made Abu Ayyub and his wife very uncomfortable—they could not imagine occupying the higher floor of the house, walking and sleeping above the Prophet (s). "How can we walk on top of the Messenger of Allah (s)? Do we come between him and the revelation? If so, how rude we must be!"

They compromised by walking only on the edges of the upper rooms and sleeping on a side of the building that was not directly above the Prophet's quarters. They carried on this way for a few days, until one night, a water jar broke on the floor. The couple panicked, fearing that water would drip down on the Prophet (s). They grabbed their only velvet blanket and used it to mop up the water. The next morning, Abu Ayyub confessed how awkward and sleepless their nights had been, due to sleeping above the Prophet (s). So Prophet Muhammad (s) agreed to take the second floor.

● ● ● Two Brothers' Creativity

Once the grandsons of the Prophet (s), al-Hasan and al-Hussein, noticed a man who was making *wudu* incorrectly. Because they were young and the man was older, they wanted to correct him in a way that was most courteous and would not bring about any embarrassment. They approached the man and said, "Uncle, will you help us? My brother and I are arguing about who makes the best *wudu*, and I swear I make it just like the Prophet (s) did." The man agreed cheerfully to arbitrate between the two young men.

So the first one made *wudu*, perfecting every step. Then his brother made *wudu*, exactly the same, perfecting each movement. The man was amazed. When they had both completed *wudu*, they turned to the man to hear his reaction. The old man smiled and said, "No, I've learned today that I am the one who was not perfecting his *wudu*, and you two have taught me how to perfect it."

• • • Courtesy in the Face of Rudeness

During the 13 years that the Prophet (s) invited people to Islam in Makkah, he had to deal with so much insult and rudeness from his people. One example of the Prophet's extreme courtesy and patience is his conversation with Utbah ibn Rabee' in the 3rd or 4th year of prophethood.

Utbah was a skilled orator and politician—he often served as Quraish's ambassador to foreign rulers. He knew how to sweet talk and persuade, and he also knew how to give veiled insults. Quraish appointed him to go to the Prophet (s) and attempt to negotiate with him. Utbah asked to speak with the Prophet (s), and the Prophet (s), undoubtedly knowing what would be said, still gave the man his full attention. Utbah said, "Cousin, you had a high position amongst us, in influence, tribal connections and kinship. But you brought something that disunited your people and split apart our families. You denounce our gods, and you claim to be better than your ancestors. We have a proposition for you, and I warn you to think well before you reject it."

The Prophet (s) responded patiently, "I am listening to you, Abu al-Waleed."

Utbah then continued to bribe the Prophet (s) with wealth, kingdom, cure for his sickness (as if calling to Islam was a sickness), and women. In the face of these veiled insults, the Prophet (s) listened quietly and attentively, without any sign of impatience. When Utbah finished, the Prophet (s) said, "Are you done Abu al-Waleed? Now listen to me."

The Prophet (s) began with "*Bismillah ar-Rahman ar-Raheem*," and proceeded to recite the first 13 verses of *Surah Fussilat*. When he reached the verse, "But if they turn away, then say, "I have warned you of a thunderbolt like the thunderbolt which struck Aad and Thamud..." (41:13) Utbah flew into a panic and put his hands on the mouth of the Prophet (s), asking him to stop. The Prophet (s) said, "Abu al-Waleed, you have heard what I recited, and you may respond as you like." Utbah returned to Quraish, who were awaiting the results of the negotiation. When they saw him, they noticed his face had changed dramatically. They asked him what had happened. Utbah replied, "By Allah, I've heard words unlike any before. They were not lines of poetry, magic, or any such thing..."

• • • Oops, I forgot!

Anas ibn Malik would grow up to be a great
Companion, but at the time of this story he was a
boy about ten years old. When Prophet Muhammad
(s) migrated to Madinah, Anas' mother, Um Sulaim,
dedicated her son to the service of the Prophet (s)
and wished that he spend all of his time close to the
Prophet (s). One day, the Prophet (s) asked Anas to do
an errand. Anas set out, determined to do what the
Prophet asked. On his way, he came across his friends
playing. They were having so much fun! Anas joined
the play for a little while, and soon he had forgotten
about the Prophet's errand. Suddenly, he felt a hand
on his back. He spun around to see the Prophet
smiling at him. He (s) said, "Unais (little Anas), did
you forget to go where I asked?" Anas immediately
responded, "Yes! I am going!" Many years later, Anas
would recall, "I served the Prophet for nine years. Not
once did he scold me, asking me why I did or didn't
do something." (Muslim)

• • • True Value

At the time of the Prophet (s), there was a bedouin man named Zahir ibn Hizam. He was generally unattractive, lonely, and unliked. One day, Zahir was trying to sell goods in the market and the Prophet (s) came up behind him and embraced him from behind (or put his hands over Zahir's eyes). Zahir became angry and shouted, "Who is it?" He spun around and immediately softened when he found the Prophet's smiling face. The Prophet (s) took the arm of Zahir and held it up in the market, as a joke, and said, "Who would like to buy this servant from me?" Zahir said, "Messenger of Allah, no one would ever want to buy me—I am spoiled goods." The Prophet (s), "But you are valuable to Allah." On another occasion, the Prophet (s) said about Zahir, "Zahir is our man in the desert, and we are his town people." (al-Bayhaqi, al-Hakam)

• • • Distressed Creatures

Ibn Masud tells a story about a time when they were on a journey with the Prophet (s). They found a place to camp and the Prophet (s) wandered off. The Companions found a bird's nest and started playing with the baby birds. The mother bird came back, flying and chirping frantically. When the Prophet (s) returned, he exclaimed, "Who has made this bird so upset? Return her babies to her." Then the Prophet (s) saw that a fire had been kindled upon an ant hill. He said, "Who is burning this ant hill? Only the Lord of Fire can torment with fire." (Abu Dawud)

• • • A Thirsty Dog

Prophet Muhammad (s) said, "A man was traveling and was overwhelmed by extreme thirst. Soon he found a well, climbed down into it and drank the cool water. When he came out, he found a dog panting from thirst and licking the ground. The man said, "This dog is as thirsty as I was." And so he climbed down into the well, filled his shoe with water, and held it in his mouth as he climbed up the well. Then he gave the dog a drink from his shoe. Allah appreciated this deed, so he forgave him." The Companions said, "Messenger of Allah, is there a reward for kindness even to the animals?" The Prophet (s) said, "Yes, there is reward in serving every living creature." (Bukhari)

• • • Muawiyah's Prayer Mistake

Muawiyah ibn al-Hakam relates this story, which happened while he was new to Islam. "Once I was praying behind the Prophet (s) when a man in the congregation sneezed. So, while I was praying, I said the typical response to a sneeze, "*Yarhamak Allah* (Allah have mercy on you)." Everyone gave me strange looks, so I said, still in my prayer, "What's your problem? Why are you all looking at me?" People started to slap their thighs with their hands to make me be quiet, so I stayed quiet. After the prayer, may my mother and father be sacrificed for him, I never saw a teacher so excellent as the Prophet. By Allah he did not scold me or hit me or ridicule me. He said gently, 'In this prayer, it is not appropriate to say any normal speech. But it is only for *tasbeeh, takbeer,* and recitation of the Quran." (Abu Dawud)

• • • A Verse that Worried the Companions

When verse 284 of *Surah al-Baqarah* was revealed, it
caused the Muslims a lot of distress and worry. The
verse was as follows: "To Allah belongs whatever is in
the heavens and whatever is on the earth. Whether
you reveal what is in your hearts or conceal it, Allah
will call you to account for it. He forgives whomever
He wills, and punishes whomever He wills. And Allah
is Most Capable of everything." (2:284) The Muslims
wondered: if Allah holds us to account for what we
hide in our hearts, how can we ever be good enough?
All of us have evil thoughts sometimes and all of us
think things that we don't act upon. This weighed very
heavily on their minds.

The Companions went to the Prophet (s) and asked
him about it. They said, "Prophet of Allah, we are able
to do the duties we were prescribed, like fasting,
prayer, and charity. But then this verse was revealed
and it is too much for us."

The Prophet (s) responded, "Do you mean to say what
the people of the two books said before you when they
said, 'We hear and we disobey'? Rather you should
say, 'We hear and we obey, Your Forgiveness our Lord!
And to You is the return.'" So the Companions did as

the Prophet (s) said. After they had submitted, their hearts at ease after obeying the command of Allah in this way, Allah revealed the following verses describing the supplication of the believers and easing the worry that was in their hearts and minds. Allah said in those verses, "Allah does not require of any soul more than what it can afford. All good will be for its own benefit, and all evil will be to its own loss. The believers pray, "Our Lord! Do not punish us if we forget or make a mistake. Our Lord! Do not place a burden on us like the one you placed on those before us. Our Lord! Do not burden us with what we cannot bear. Pardon us, forgive us, and have mercy on us. You are our only Guardian. So grant us victory over the disbelieving people." (2:286)

• • • Racing to Obey

In Madinah, the Muslim community received many commands from Allah, including changes they had to make in their lifestyle and manners. The believers always hastened to implement these commands as quickly and obediently as they could.

When the final command to stop drinking alcohol came, people went to their homes and immediately broke the jars holding any alcohol and dumped whatever they had into the streets. It was said that the streets of Madinah flowed with alcohol as the entire community washed its hands of intoxicants. Similarly, when Allah gave the command for Muslim women to wear hijab, they immediately draped themselves in whatever clothing or fabric they had—tearing their aprons so as to wear them to cover their heads and chests—so that it was said that they looked like crows when they came out of their homes.

• • • The Archers at Uhud

In the Battle of Uhud, the leaders of Quraish, angry at their defeat the previous year at Badr, rallied 3,000 well-equipped soldiers and horsemen and aimed to attack the new community in Madinah. After consulting on whether to remain in Madinah and defend the city or march out to meet the army, the Prophet (s) took the advice of his Companions and marched with 1,000 Muslim soldiers to meet the approaching army.

The Muslims carefully laid the plan for the battlefield. It was essential that one of the hills around the battlefield be guarded by a squad of 50 archers, since the Muslim flank could easily be attacked from that angle by cavalry. The Prophet (s) instructed the band of archers to remain at their post no matter what—even if they saw the Muslims being defeated and even if it appeared that the battle was over.

The first half of the Battle of Uhud seemed an easy victory. Despite their greater numbers and superior equipment, the Makkan army could not stand up to the bravery of the Muslim army. Soon, the Makkan soldiers were retreating from the battlefield, and the Muslim soldiers started collecting the spoils of war left behind.

This created a dilemma among the archers. It seemed apparent that the battle was over, and they watched in disappointment as the other soldiers started collecting the riches and the spoils left behind. Standing on the mountain doing nothing, they wondered if there would be anything left for them. A group of them decided to go down and join the other soldiers. Only a few staunch souls remembered the strong instructions of the Prophet (s) and remained at their post.

Khalid ibn al-Walid, who had not yet become Muslim and was one of the Makkan army leaders, was still surveying the battlefield, looking for any way to reverse their defeat, when he saw the archers leaving the hill. This was his chance! He gathered his horsemen, and they maneuvered around the hill, killing the few remaining archers and charging down upon the Muslim army from behind. The Makkan soldiers saw this happening and launched a new attack on the disoriented Muslim army.

Many Muslims died at Uhud in the second phase of fighting. The Prophet (s) was left unguarded, save for a few Companions who happened to be near him, and he himself was seriously injured. The Muslims learned many lessons that day at the Battle of Uhud, including the importance of obedience to Allah, the Prophet (s), and leadership on the battlefield and beyond.

• • • A Stubborn Boulder

During the Battle of the Trench, the Muslims of Madinah had to dig a deep and wide trench, more than a mile long in just a few days. It was arduous, backbreaking work during the winter months, when there was little food in the city. People were hungry, scared, and exhausted. The Prophet (s) worked alongside the Companions, cheerfully doing the most difficult jobs. In order to encourage his Companions, he would chant along with the others a song composed by Abdullah ibn Rawahah:

> *O Allah, were it not for You,*
> *We would never have been guided,*

Nor have given charity, nor prayed.
So send down calmness upon us.

While they were working, the Companions came upon a huge boulder that they could not lift or break with their shovels. They called upon the Prophet (s) for help. He struck the rock three times, and each time he would strike it, a bright light would spark. With a spirit of optimism and courage, he struck the rock and shouted, "Allah is the Greatest! The keys of Syria are granted to me! I swear by Allah I can see its palaces before my eyes!" He struck it again and exclaimed, "Allah is the Greatest! Persia is granted to me! I swear by Allah I see the white palace of Mada'in." On the third strike he said, "Allah is the Greatest! I have been given the keys of Yemen! I swear by Allah I can see the gates of San'aa before me right now." Heartened by the courage and optimism of the Prophet (s) the Companions carried on with their work and completed the digging of the entire trench just in time before the armies of Arabia arrived on the edges of Madinah.

• • • A Boy and his Sparrow

At the time of the Prophet (s), there was a young boy named Zaid ibn Sahl. His nickname was Abu Umair, and he was around 4 years old. He was always found playing with his pet sparrow, al-Nughair, whom he loved a lot. Even though the Prophet (s) was the most busy and important man in Madinah, he (s) always stopped to play with Abu Umair whenever he saw him. The Prophet (s) would pause whatever he was doing and would cheerfully play with the little boy. One day, the Prophet (s) found the little boy looking sad. When he asked why, he was told the boy's pet sparrow had died. As always, the Prophet (s) paused what he was doing. He gently asked, "Abu Umair, what happened to little Nughair?" The Prophet (s) sat with the little boy and distracted him until he cheered up.

••• Incredible Management

One day the King of Egypt had a dream. He said, "I saw seven fat cows being eaten by seven that were lean, and I saw seven green stalks of grain overcome by seven that were dry and ready for harvesting. Oh my advisors, tell me, if you know, what does this mean." Prophet Yousef interpreted this dream and suggested the solution. He said, "The next seven years will be abundant with lots of food for eating. Then there will be seven years of drought, and if you don't prepare, the people will be starving. So for the next seven years, leave what you harvest in its husk and store it, except for the little you need for eating." Prophet Yusuf was able to save not only the people of Egypt, but the entire region from starvation. Imagine the amount of planning, logistics, calculations and management that Yusuf had to execute in order to manage this massive operation.

• • • Whatever you want, you buy?

Umar ibn Al-Khattab once observed Jabir ibn Abdallah holding some money in his hand and asked where he was headed. Jabir said that he was off to buy some meat for his family because they desired it. Upon this, Umar exclaimed incredulously, "Whatever you desire, you buy?! Do you fill your belly apart from your cousin and your neighbor? What about the verse, "You squandered the good things you were given in your earthly life, you took your fill of pleasure there..." [46:20] Jabir later said, "I wish the money had fallen from my hand, and I had not run into Umar!"

••• A Delicious Meal at Abu Ayyoob's

The Prophet (s) came out to the mosque one day in the
scorching midday heat, a time that most people would
use for a short nap, and found Abu Bakr and Umar
there. "What is it that brings you both out of your
houses at this time?" he asked. "Hunger, Messenger
of Allah," they replied in desperation. The Prophet
(s) admitted that it was the same pain that kept him
from being able to rest, and so they went to visit Abu
Ayyoob, a man from the Ansar who used to take great
pleasure in sharing what he had with the Prophet (s)
and always had some food and milk set aside for him.

When they reached Abu Ayyoob's door, his wife came
out and said, "Welcome, O Prophet of Allah and those
who are with him!" The Prophet (s) asked her, "Where
is Abu Ayyoob?" Abu Ayyoob had heard the voice of the
Prophet (s) as he was working in his date plantation, so
he came running. He said, "Welcome, Prophet of Allah
and those who are with him!" Then, abashed for not
having his usual preparations ready for the Prophet's
(s) arrival, he said, "O Prophet of Allah, this is not the
usual time that you would come." The Prophet (s) said,
"That is true."

Abu Ayoob went out and cut a bunch of dates from the palm trees, containing all kinds of dry, moist, and green dates. The Prophet (s) said, "I didn't intend this. You should have just picked the dry ones for us." He said, "O Prophet of Allah, I wanted you to eat from the dry, the moist, and the green ones. I will also bring some meat for you in addition to this." He said, "If you do slaughter, then do not slaughter the one with milk." He then took a young female or male goat and slaughtered it. He said to his wife, "Bake some dough for us, for you are better at baking." He took the goat and grilled half of it.

When the food was ready, he placed it before the Prophet (s) and his Companions. The Prophet (s) then took some of the goat and placed it in a loaf of bread. He said, "O Abu Ayyoob, send this to Fatimah, for she has not had anything like this for days." Abu Ayyoob sent the package of food to the daughter of the Prophet (s).

After they ate and were satisfied, the Prophet (s) said, "Bread, meat, dry dates, green dates, and moist dates!" as his eyes teared. "I swear by the One in whose hand is my soul, these are certainly the pleasures about which you will be asked!" and then he quoted the verse in *Surah al-Takāthur*, "These are certainly the pleasures about which you will be asked on the Day of Resurrection."

That worried his Companions greatly, for they now felt guilty for indulging in what, to them, seemed like an unjustifiable luxury. The Prophet (s) noticed their dismay, and so he instructed them to say "In the name of Allah" (*bismillāh*) before they eat, and afterwards, "All praise is due to Allah, who was the One who satisfied us, blessed us, and was generous to us." (*al-hamdu lillâh il-ladhi huwa ashba'anâ wa an'ama 'alaynâ wa afdhal*). He told them, "This would suffice as a response."

• • • Standing up to the Byzantine Emperor

Twice in his lifetime, Abdullah ibn Huthafah stood bravely before a powerful emperor, inviting to Islam, standing up for his faith, and never flinching—once as the Prophet's messenger to the emperor of Persia and the second time as a captive before the Roman Emperor. When the Roman emperor found out they had captured a group of Muslim soldiers, he inquired if there were any Companions of the Prophet (s) among them. The emperor had heard so much about the bravery and sincerity of the Companions that he was determined to turn one of them away from his faith so he could brag about it. It so happened that the Companion they found among the captives was Abdullah ibn Huthafah.

Bound in chains and exhausted from the journey, Abdullah was brought before the emperor. The emperor tempted him with every possible comfort and luxury in exchange for leaving Islam: wealth, kingdoms, palaces, even the princess's hand in marriage. Imagine what this weary soldier must have felt—thinking he would be killed immediately but instead being offered the highest positions in the land! Abdullah turned it all down—he would not choose anything over Allah.

Realizing that bribery wouldn't work, the emperor ordered a huge cauldron full of oil to be brought forth. Abdullah looked on as they heated the oil until it began to boil and spatter. They brought another Muslim captive and threw his body into the oil. Can you imagine what a terrible scene that was and what Abdullah must have felt being forced to watch? The flesh was fried off the soldier's body until there was nothing left but bones. Yet Abdullah was firm. When the emperor asked if he would prefer to have his flesh boiled in oil, Abdullah said he would never leave Islam, even if it came to that.

So the emperor ordered that Abdullah be thrown into the oil. As his men led the captive to the cauldron, the emperor noticed tears on Abdullah's face. He stopped his men, hoping eagerly that Abdullah had changed his mind. When he was asked the reason for his tears, Abdullah answered, "By Allah, I wasn't crying because I was afraid of dying. No, I cried because I only have one soul to give to Allah, and I would have loved to have 100 lives so I could give all of them for the sake of Allah."

The emperor was astonished beyond words. Abdullah's faith and bravery impressed him so much that he made one more offer—he would release Abdullah and all the Muslim prisoners of war if only Abdullah would kiss the emperor's forehead. Abdullah ibn Huthafah thought for a moment. It was a small act, one that involved no disbelief nor sin, and one that would save the lives of his fellow soldiers. So Abdullah kissed the man's forehead, and the Muslims were freed.

When they reached Madinah, Abdullah narrated the entire story to Umar ibn al-Khattab. When Abdullah finished the story, Umar said, "It is a duty for every Muslim to kiss the head of this man, Abdullah ibn Huthafah, and I will be the first one to do so."

• • • Strength of Two Words

Bilal was an Abyssinian man in Makkah when the call to Islam was new and just becoming known. He was also a slave, and his master Umayyah ibn Khalaf was one of the most vicious opponents of Islam. Still, Bilal did not hesitate to embrace Islam as soon as he heard its message.

Umayyah ibn Khalaf and his henchmen proceeded to heap torture and torment on Bilal. Bilal had no family or tribe to protect him so he was an easy target. They would tie him up, taunt him, beat him, and deprive him of food and water. During these terrible times of pain and ridicule, Bilal would derive strength from saying, "Ahad, Ahad—One, One." Later, when asked why this was the phrase he chose, wise Bilal would say, "That was what I knew about Allah. If I had known anything else, I would have said more."

The torture escalated. They would drag Bilal out to the desert, lay him on the scorching sand under the blazing sun, and order the other slaves to roll a huge boulder onto his chest. Bilal would fade in and out of consciousness, repeating the words, "Ahad, Ahad..." This drove the leaders of Quraish mad. In this way, a weak slave became one of the strongest men, deriving his strength directly from Allah.

Eventually, Abu Bakr intervened, fearing that Bilal would not survive the torture. "How much do you want for him?" Abu Bakr asked Umayyah. Umayyah asked for 10 dinars, which was considered a very high price at the time for a slave. Abu Bakr did not argue and promptly paid the price. Umayyah laughed and said, "If you had negotiated, I would have given him to you for just one dinar." Abu Bakr retorted, "And if you had set the price of his freedom at 100 dinars, I would still have paid the price!"

• • • Lady of the Two Waistbands

During the Prophet's migration to Madinah, help was needed to ensure that the journey was carried out safely and secretly. The Prophet (s) and Abu Bakr depended on a few individuals to support them and keep the arrangements secret—including Asma, the daughter of Abu Bakr.

Because there were armed search parties and assassins prowling the desert, the Prophet (s) and Abu Bakr headed south instead of north and hid in a cave for a few days until the search campaign died down. Asma knew the location of the cave where the Prophet (s) and her father hid. Pregnant and alone, she made the 3-mile trip back and forth through the desert carrying food and supplies.

On her way, she was unable to carry all of the supplies and so untied her waistband, tore it in half, and used it to hold and tie all that she had to carry. When the Prophet (s) saw this, he gave her the nickname she is well-known for until today, "*Thaat an-Nitaqayn*" or Lady of the Two Waistbands.

Enemies would knock on the door of Asma, demanding to know where the Prophet (s) was. She was brave and resolute in the face of their anger. One day, Abu Jahl, one of the most formidable enemies of Islam, lost his temper when she refused to tell him what she knew. He slapped her across her face so hard that her earring tore through her earlobe. Still, she did not yield. Several weeks later, Asma followed the Prophet (s) and her father to Madinah. Immediately upon arriving, she gave birth to one of the great heroes of Islam, Abdullah ibn az-Zubair.

• • • A Loud Noise in Madinah

Anas ibn Malik described the bravery of the Prophet (s) during a scary incident in Madinah. One night the people heard a loud, strange noise outside of the city– unlike anything they had ever heard before. They came together and walked towards the noise, cautious and fearful. On their way to the location of the mysterious noise, they saw a figure walking toward them in the dark. As it approached, they realized it was the Prophet (s) on horseback, carrying his sword. He had been the first to run out into the desert to scout out the cause of the noise. He reassured the people, saying, "No cause for fear. Do not be afraid." (Bukhari and Muslim)

Mystery of the Man of Paradise

Once some of the Companions were sitting with the Prophet (s). He announced, "Coming upon you now is a man from the people of Paradise." A man from the Ansar entered—his beard was disheveled by the water of ablution, and he carried both of his shoes in his left hand. The Companions did not see anything exceptional about this man and wondered what he did that made him a person of Paradise. The next day the Prophet (s) repeated the same words, and there he was! The same man, entering upon them in the same manner.

On the third day when the same thing happened again, Abdullah ibn Umar decided to get to the bottom of the story. He visited the man and pretended that he had a disagreement with his father and needed a place to stay for three days. The man from the Ansar welcomed him into his home.

Abdullah stayed three nights with the man but did not notice anything exceptional. The man did not pray at night—whenever he went to bed, he would remember Allah and then sleep until he woke up for the morning prayer. He spoke only good, kind words, but Abdullah was still puzzled. He could not understand what deed had earned him a guaranteed place in Paradise.

Finally, Abdullah confessed to the man. He said, "I actually have not had a disagreement with my father and am in good relations with him. But the Prophet (s) said three times that a man from the people of Paradise would come through the door, and it was you! I stayed with you so that I could find out what your secret was, so I could learn and do the same thing, but I didn't observe you doing anything special. Why did the Prophet (s) speak so highly of you?"

The man thought for a moment and said, "I am as you have seen."

Abdullah was about to leave without an answer to his question, but finally the man spoke again. He said, "I am as you have seen, except that I have no resentment in my soul towards the Muslims, and I do not envy the good that Allah has given anyone." Realizing that this was the answer to the puzzle, Abdullah responded, "This is what you have achieved, and it is something we have not accomplished." Abdullah realized that this man managed to maintain a clean, pure heart towards all people, and that was what had earned him such a high rank. (Ahmad)

• • • The Woman who Cleaned the Mosque

There lived a poor African woman amongst the early Muslims in Madinah. She was far from her home country and family, and had no connections or status among the Arab tribes of Madinah. Her name was Umm Mihjan, and to show her love for Islam, she worked hard cleaning the mosque of the Prophet (s). She swept the sand and dust, removed debris, and maintained the mosque perfectly every day.

The Prophet (s) always greeted her, inquired about her, and honored her. When she became ill and death approached her, the Prophet (s) told the Companions who were watching over her, if she dies, tell me immediately. When she passed away, the Companions went to find the Prophet (s) but found that he had fallen asleep. Hating to wake him, they went ahead with the funeral arrangements, prayed the funeral prayer and took her to be buried.

When he awoke, the Prophet (s) asked about Umm Mihjan. The Companions gave him the sad news that she had passed away. The Prophet (s) was distressed: "Why didn't you wake me? Show me her grave." He (s) hurried toward the graveyard and when he came to her grave, he stood for prayer, and the Companions stood behind him. He (s) prayed the *janazah* prayer again on her, making four *takbirs* and a special *dua* for her. He (s) insisted on giving this humble, inconspicuous woman the same honor he gave to his greatest Companions.

• • • The Weeping Tree

Prophet Muhammad's mosque was very simple—it was an open-air space, shaded with tree branches and surrounded by clay bricks. Inside the mosque there was a palm tree, which the Prophet (s) used to lean on while he was giving the Friday khutbah. One of the women of the Ansar asked that a pulpit be crafted so that the Prophet (s) could be seen and his voice heard more easily. The Prophet (s) agreed, and the Companions built him a simple pulpit with three steps.

The following Friday, the Prophet (s) climbed up the new pulpit. But something very unexpected happened—everyone in the mosque heard a weeping and moaning sound, so loud that the mosque shook. The strange sound was coming from the tree that the Prophet (s) used to lean on. It wept because it no longer could be close to the Prophet (s), and it wept because it loved to hear the verses of Allah at its side. Even Allah's creations in nature feel a reverence toward Allah and the Prophet (s).

As everyone looked on, and as the moaning continued, the Prophet (s) climbed down the pulpit and put his hand on the tree and hugged it until it quieted. When the tree died many years later, the Companions buried it in the ground—the famous tree that wept because it loved and revered the Prophet (s).

••• The Mindful Milkmaid

When Umar became the ruler of the Muslims, he was extremely worried that he would unknowingly neglect some of his people. After his governing responsibilities were over, he would spend his hours—not enjoying himself or relaxing—but wandering the streets and outskirts of the city, often with Ibn Abbas or another Companion, searching for those who were suffering in silence. There are many stories about the people and situations Umar encountered during these rounds.

While passing by one of the poor homes, Umar heard whispering inside. A mother was giving some advice to her daughter: "We didn't sell enough milk today. When

I was younger, I used to add some water to the milk so that I would have more to sell. Let's do that now."

The daughter objected. "But that was before you were Muslim. Now that we are Muslim, we can't do that. The Caliph Umar has forbidden mixing water with milk."

"Umar is not here right now! And what are we supposed to do? Starve?"

The girl was insistent. "The Caliph may not be here, but we must obey his order. Even if we can escape the notice of the Caliph, we cannot escape the notice of Allah."

Umar marveled at this girl's reverence and determination to obey Allah. The next day, he sent someone to buy the milk from the two milkmaids, and they found the milk was pure with no water added. The girl had succeeded in persuading her mother not to add the water.

Realizing the treasure this girl contained in her heart, Umar summoned the mother and her daughter. He also invited his sons, and asked one of them to marry the young milkmaid. Umar's son Asim readily accepted, and this young woman became the daughter-in-law of the Caliph. She would bear a daughter, named Um Asim, and Um Asim would be the mother of one of the greatest rulers of Islam, the fifth righteous Caliph Umar ibn Abdul Azeez.

• • • • Standing for a Jewish Funeral

In Madinah, the Prophet (s) ensured that people of all religions were able to live in peace and practice their faith. One of the first things he did upon arriving in Madinah was draft a constitution, or the "*Saheefah*." This *Saheefah* declared that all of the inhabitants of Madinah, whether Jews, Christians, or other faiths, were considered citizens of Madinah, regardless of religion, race or ancestry. Regarding the Jews, the *Saheefah* said, "To the Jews who ally with us, they have our help and equity. They shall not be harmed nor their enemies aided against them."

An example of the respect shown to people of other religions is an instance when the Prophet (s) was seated with his Companions, and a Jewish funeral procession passed by. The Prophet (s) stood up. One of the Companions did not understand and asked why the Prophet (s) was standing for a Jew—this was not a Muslim funeral procession! The Prophet (s) corrected them by saying, "Is he not a human being?"

About the Author

Younoos Latheef has 20+ years of experience servicing the Houston Muslim community, including leadership positions within MAS Scouts and MAS Youth. He currently serves as the chaplain advisor for MAS Scouting Unit 713 in Houston, Texas. In his book, Cultivating Character, he leverages his experience to share a practical guide to instilling Islam in scouting or youth group curricula. By trade, he is a change management professional and holds an MBA from the University of Texas at Austin.